Death & Taxes

HYDRIOTAPHIA & OTHER PLAYS

Tony Kushner

THEATRE COMMUNICATIONS GROUP

Death & Taxes: Hydriotaphia & Other Plays is published by
Theatre Communications Group, Inc., 355 Lexington Ave.,
New York, NY 10017–6603.

This publication is made possible in part with public funds from the New York State Council on the Arts, a State Agency.

TCG books are exclusively distributed to the book trade by Consortium Book Sales and Distribution, 1045 Westgate Dr., St. Paul, MN 55114.

LIBRARY OF CONGRESS CATALOGING-IN-PUBLICATION DATA
Kushner, Tony.
Death and Taxes : Hydriotaphia, and other plays / by Tony Kushner. — 1st ed.
p. cm.
ISBN 1-55936-156-5 (alk. paper)
I. Title.
PS3561.U778 D4 1998
812'.54—dc21 98-49486
CIP

Book design and typography by Lisa Govan
Cover design by Cynthia Krupat
Cover woodcut by Hans Holbein the Younger

First edition, June 2000

Death & Taxes

HYDRIOTAPHIA & OTHER PLAYS

. . . poems should be written
rarely and reluctantly,
under unbearable duress
and only with the hope
that good spirits, not evil ones,
choose us for their instruments.

—CZESLAW MILOSZ
from "Ars Poetica?"

Table of Contents

Thanks as always to Terry Nemeth, patron saint of play publishing, and again to Kathy Sova, for their patience and thoughtful guidance; to Joyce Ketay, as always my wonder-agent and fellow adventurer; and to Mark Harris, with love and gratitude for reading the contents of this book and helping me groom it.

Introduction

. . . In vain do individuals hope for immortality,
or any patent from oblivion,
in preservations below the Moon . . .

from "Hydriotaphia or Urne-Buriall"
—SIR THOMAS BROWNE

THIS IS AN ODD assemblage of plays, for which gathering-together there is no overarching thematic justification. Because several of the plays deal with death, and one of the death-plays deals as well with money, and the last play deals with taxation, we're calling the book *Death & Taxes.* But all plays, directly or indirectly, are about death and taxes, so this title explains little. I could have called it *Things I Wrote While Mustering the Courage to Write a Full-length Play to Follow Angels in America*, and that would have been more precise, but also misleading, since I have written a few full-length plays since *Angels*, which are being nursed to viability and presentability in various incubatory and preparatory institutions, soon (if my courage holds up) to be released for public viewing, and the devil take the hindmost. I don't have a real job but my not-real job is tough, at least it is tough for an essentially lily-livered person such as my timorous self.

I wrote *Reverse Transcription* because Michael Bigelow Dixon, the dramaturgical eminence of the Actors Theatre of Louisville, asked me to write a ten-minute play. It was produced in 1996 at the Humana Festival, which is a sort of beauty pageant for new plays, where it was entirely outshone by another ten-minute play, *What I Meant Was*, a tiny masterpiece by Craig Lucas, to whom, coincidentally, *Reverse Transcription* is dedicated.

Scott Cummings, drama critic for the *Boston Phoenix,* approached me in the ATL bar after a performance with the theory that *Reverse Transcription* is a personal lament for writing in a quieter, safer time, before all the hoo-hah over *Angels*. Scott pointed out that Ding, the name of the play's deceased playwright, is the sound a typewriter carriage makes on its return—an evocation, he proposed, of an earlier (pre-word-processor) day and age, before writing became so electrified, so scary. "And poor Ding is dead."

My favorite part of the play is Ella Fitzgerald's *Cole Porter Songbook* version of "Begin the Beguine," the first Tin Pan Alley tune I ever memorized (the start of a lifelong addiction), which I sing to myself for good luck before every opening night, which I have stipulated in my will is to be played at my funeral, along with Mahler's "Resurrection" Symphony, Dvořák's Ninth, Brahms's Fourth and Bach's St. Matthew's Passion. I envision a lengthy service. Bring lunch.

I have always told people that my first play was *A Bright Room Called Day*, and my second play was *Angels in America, Part One: Millennium Approaches.* This is, as Rudolph Giuliani, Mayor of New York, once put it, "so far from the truth that it is almost a lie." In between writing *Bright Room* and *Angels*, I wrote another play, a weird one, called *Hydriotaphia or The Death of Dr. Browne.* Though I didn't realize it at the time, I think I wrote *Hydriotaphia* as a crash course in learning how to write jokes. I assembled a cast before I started writing—friends, actors I'd met while doing graduate work at

New York University's Theater Program—so each part was written for a specific personality. The play starred Stephen Spinella, my favorite actor on earth, and many other spectacularly talented people. I wrote it in three weeks, and we spent three weeks rehearsing it, and we performed it, all three hours of it, in a tiny un-air-conditioned theater in Soho in full period costumes (scrabbled together from cheesecloth, mop handles and moth-eaten bathrobes on a $1,000 budget by the astounding Priscilla Stampa, who also triumphed as the ancient cook, Babbo) during a month-long lethal heat wave, in the summer of 1987, featuring on-the-street temperatures of 102 degrees and in-the-theater temperatures of at least twice that. The cast and I loved working on *Hydriotaphia*, loved performing it. Its audiences were confused by it, mostly; they were being baked, they were oxygen-deprived, they were perched on metal folding chairs, they were baffled by everything from the made-up dialect the servants speak to the play's title. People left silently, slick with sweat, weak with heat exhaustion and relief. I was devastated. The director, Michael Greif, who came up to me after one especially grim, sweltering performance, shoved both his hands in my hair, rubbed vigorously as if doing a phrenological exam, and said, "You have a good head." It was exactly what I needed to hear, and it remains perhaps the most reassuring compliment I have ever received. It's not especially reassuring to be praised extravagantly, as it tends to make one, well, to make *me* feel fraudulent, but it is nice, and not excessively productive of cognitive dissonance, to be told you have a good head. I am grateful to Michael to this day.

I first read Thomas Browne's essay, "Hydriotaphia or Urne-Buriall" because, years ago, when I was a student at Columbia University, a boy I was in love with, a Harvard student, had memorized several passages from the essay to declaim at some ancient declamation competition Harvard annually sponsors. He was lovely and he had a deep, velvety voice, my beloved, a marvelous purr, perfect for the churchyard-tolling cadences and sepulchral mysteries of Browne's intricately twisted black coral branch of a prose poem. I was so afraid of my sexual feelings at that time, locked so tightly in my closet, I didn't realize I was painfully in love. This is the keenest memory from my time adoring Jim: Him standing in his dorm room, me lying on his bed, rapturously listening to him, his sonorous, sexy recitation of Browne's three-hundred-plus-years-old brooding on the subject of death and life-after-death. Love denied, seeking attachment, will fall in love with its own funeral service; mine did.

After the first production, I shoved *Hydriotaphia* in my file cabinet, and it would have remained there, I think, probably permanently. But Michael Mayer, my best girlfriend, now a fabulous director, who was the assistant director and stage manager for the original production, asked me to let him have a go at *Hydriotaphia* as a project for graduate students at NYU in 1998, eleven years after the original production. I rewrote some of it, but most of the present version, and the play's essential weirdness, remain unchanged from the first draft. Michael Mayer got too busy to continue with the project at NYU, so Michael Wilson took over, and with a marvelous student cast did a marvelous job staging the play; which he then brought to the Alley Theatre in Houston. The Houston audiences were largely annoyed by what they saw, and they had *plush seats and lots of air-conditioning*; when the production moved on to Berkeley Rep, audiences were more enthusiastic, but not much more. Critics sniffed.

I have hopes that *Hydriotaphia* will find its production and its audience somewhere, someday. Perhaps the play is more comfortable in the improvisational, impoverished circumstances whence it sprang, minus the punishing heat wave. Plays retain, as if holding a deep memory, the conditions and occasions of their creation; the origins haunt future productions of any given play, even when the play is very old. The original event is worked into the lines, into the stage directions if there are any, into the rhythms of the text, like a trauma; the restless spirit of the first production stirs each time the text is brought into rehearsal.

The actor who first played Death, Sam Calandrino, completely terrifying and delightful in the part, died immediately after the production, following complications from an emergency surgery.

G. David Schine in Hell was written in 1996 for the *New York Times Magazine* as part of their year-end roundup of deceased notable Americans. Because of strict *Times'* policies, much of the profanity in the piece had to be edited out. I argued this policy over the phone with a beleaguered copy editor. I was in the lobby of a small hotel on the Yorkshire moors, and I heatedly defended each "FUCK" in the piece, not realizing that I was offending the other hotel guests, until a pleasant but insistent assistant manager requested that I hang up the pay phone and leave the establishment. I was amused that the *Times* would not allow the term "alter kocher," which means "old-timer," because it is literally but inaccurately translated as "old crapper"; on the other hand, "dreck," which actually *means* "shit" and is frequently used to mean "shit," had been used six times previously in the newspaper, so it was ruled that "dreck" was permissible. The copy editor, who the week before had had to edit out the expletives in a lengthy article about the Attica uprising, was pleasant and consoling, but not especially impressed by nor sympathetic to my complaints.

Notes on Akiba was written on an airplane in 1995 for an event at the Jewish Museum, The Third Seder, sponsored by the great klezmer band, The Klezmatics. Michael Mayer, my best girlfriend, and I performed it, lashing each other with leeks.

Terminating was commissioned in 1998 by The Acting Company to be part of an omnibus play called "Love's Fire," conceived by Anne Cattaneo as a series of one-acts based on Shakespeare's sonnets. I love the sonnets but I have always found that the love object remains rather generic throughout, and only the sonneteer, the lover, is illuminated, revealed—this may say something about love as a primarily narcissistic enterprise; I reject that premise. The sonnets, read back-to-back, call to mind a brilliant obsessive, hammering hammering hammering away at some other person, the adored, who never gets a word in and, finally, must feel rather worn out, being so much admired and inspected and derided and desired; who must, finally, many sonnets into it, wish that the adorer would put his cornucopia away and retire for the night.

Terminating or Sonnet LXXV or "Lass meine Schmerzen nicht verloren sein" or Ambivalence is dedicated to my psychoanalyst, the great Deborah Glazer, with whom, sadly, very very sadly, I am terminating, after life-changing work. Let no one ever believe that psychoanalysis, or very good therapy, is a waste of time, for to believe that is to believe that people aren't changeable, and to believe that people aren't changeable is to miss the whole point of everything, of sea-changing Shakespeare and of life and everything. "Lass meine Schmerzen nicht verloren sein" is a prayer sung by Ariadne in Strauss's *Ariadne Auf Naxos.* "Let my pain not be in vain." Sing it, sister. And how is pain redeemable? When it alters something for the better. As it sometimes can do.

The volume closes with *East Coast Ode to Howard Jarvis.* I was hired by Alec Baldwin to write a short monologue spoken by an ordinary working-class New Yorker dealing with an extraordinary situation. Instead I wrote a play of extremely short monologues spoken by many working-class New Yorkers who made an extraordinary mess and then faced the consequences. This sad story really happened, though not precisely as I have described it. I read in the papers that a bunch of cops and other law enforcement officers had gotten caught evading taxes, believing that submitting to the tax authorities a dazzlingly stupid letter/manifesto relieved them of the obligation. Their letter was quoted in full in the papers, splenetically hissing, buzzing, cackling with the rhetoric of the loony right, of militia groups and white supremacists and Trent Lott and Charlton Heston. I was curious about how New York cops had come across such a document, and I decided that it must have been found on the Internet. I was right. I assumed that citizens of my beloved city wouldn't have shared deeply the pernicious politics of those antisocial, antidemocratic, murderous nutbag groups; I assumed that the real ideologues of the violent right were still to be found mainly in places like Colorado, Texas, Idaho, Orange County, and had established no beachhead in rude-but-sane, contentious, incessantly public/civic and, basically decent, New York. And I was right again—the cops who fished the letter from the Web appear to have been driven entirely by greed, and not infected by the uglier, darker ambitions of the Reagan/Gingrich/Bush anti-tax counterrevolution. This is partly what fascinated me about the story, the way that it recapitulated the success of the right in the 1980s and 1990s, getting people to sell their birthright (a functioning pluralistic democracy) for a mess of pottage.

I should mention that this play was written in 1996, and my beloved city has changed. Recent events in the drastically polarized, bunkered and barricaded New York of Rudolph Giuliani, with its creepy cleanliness, with its union-busting, its museum-busting, its autocratic irrationality, its hate-the-poor heartlessness, with the torture of Abner Louima and the mayorally sanctioned killings of Amadou Diallo and Patrick Dorismond—this shift, these outrages, make me wonder if perhaps the more sinister aspects of the radical right's political project *have* taken root, even here; if the ego anarchism, gun fetishism, supremacism masquerading as individualism, the tyranny masquerading as moral defense and free-market frat party, have come to seem as reasonable to a sizable percentage of New Yorkers in 2000 as they seemed enticing to the sad (mostly southern and midwestern young white male) one-fifth of the national populace that voted for the Gingrich gang in 1995; if even New York is weakening in its resolve to remain multicultural, democratic, communal, free. Since New York with its vibrant, brilliant culture has always been America's proof that these social ideals are worth striving for, tough though the struggle may be, such a capitulation would be a tragedy of national proportions.

East Coast Ode has yet to be filmed. I've performed it publicly on numerous occasions, as I travel around, doing lectures and readings, earning money while avoiding writing plays. I have written a few screenplays and teleplays, including *Ode*, all languishing, none scheduled for production. Perhaps my screenplays retain as a deep memory the deep distaste their author feels for the form. I love movies, but somebody else should write them; at least I feel this way today, mostly because, though I have been handsomely remunerated for my movie and TV writing, I am bitterly disappointed, as none of my work for Hollywood has achieved what I'd hoped for it, which is to provide its author a pretext to meet Meryl Streep.

I write for film and TV to pay bills, and to pay taxes, which burden flesh is heir to, and that is that, and it's unseemly to complain. I have never been good with my money; it and I are soon parted. I have specified in my will that, on my tombstone, I want carved Blanche Dubois's line, for which wisdom either she or Tennessee ought to have received the Nobel Prize for Economics, "Money just goes, it just goes places." I don't mind being a working writer. I suspect that I would produce nothing were I not afraid of bankruptcy. What else goads us to produce, at least as our social and political economy is currently constituted, but a fear of the taxman, and a fear of death? Both death and taxes impose upon our liberty; absolute liberty, like immortality, is pure fantasy, for we are all communal, connected, contexted, and understanding our context makes the inescapable imposition of taxes, and of death, less onerous. To live forever, to be beholden to no one and responsible for nothing, to be for yourself alone —well of course all of us dream these dreams, bracing and lonely, but dreams end, and the sun comes up, and shake a leg and get to work, serious work! Tax time is nigh, and the deadline approaches.

Tony Kushner
Union Square, The Upper West Side, Manitou
April 1, 2000

Reverse Transcription

Six Playwrights Bury a Seventh

A Ten-Minute Play That's Nearly Twenty Minutes Long

This play is for Craig Lucas

Thanks to Michael Bigelow Dixon, Jon Jory, who commissioned the play, and Liz Engleman and Jeffrey Ullom, who helped me think about it; also Lisa Peterson, my dear friend, who came to rehearsal, listened, and said she didn't understand what I was going on about. The play improved as a result.

Production History

In March 1996 *Reverse Transcription* was produced by the Actors Theatre of Louisville (Jon Jory, Producing Director) as part of the Ten-Minute Play series of their 20th Annual Humana Festival of New American Plays. The production was directed by the author. Scenic design was by Paul Owen, costumes were by Kevin R. McLeod, lights were by T. J. Gerckens and sound was by Martin R. Desjardins. The cast was as follows:

HAUTFLOTE	John Leonard Thompson
ASPERA	Jennifer Hubbard
BIFF	Christopher Evan Welch
HAPPY	Daniel Oreskes
OTTOLINE	Fanni Green
FLATTY	Fred Major
DING	

Characters

HAUTFLOTE, a playwright in his late thirties. He writes beautiful plays that everyone admires; he has a following and little financial success. He was Ding's best friend, and is the executor of his will and his wishes.

ASPERA, a playwright in her early thirties. She writes fierce, splendidly intelligent, challenging plays, frequently with lesbian characters, and cannot get an American theater to produce her for love or money. So she lives in London where she is acclaimed. She is cool and is beginning to sound British.

BIFF, a playwright in his late thirties. Scruffy, bisexual, one success, several subsequent failures, cannot stay away from political themes though his analysis is not rigorous. He is overdue; he should be home writing; he should not be here.

HAPPY, a playwright in his late thirties. His early plays were widely admired, then one big success and he's become a Hollywood writer, TV mostly, rich now, a little bored, but very happy. He plans to go back to writing for the theater someday.

OTTOLINE, a playwright in her fifties. African-American, genuinely great, hugely influential experimentalist whom everyone adores but who is now languishing in relative obscurity and neglect, though she continues to write prolifically. She is the best writer of the bunch and the least well remunerated. Her's is a deep bitterness; the surface is immensely gracious. She teaches playwrights and has a zoological fascination, watching them. Ding was her protégé, sort of. She is an old friend of Flatty's.

FLATTY, a playwright in his late forties. Colossally rich. An easy target for negativity of all kinds, though he is in fact a good writer, hugely prolific, very hard-working and generous to his fellow playwrights.

DING, a dead playwright wrapped in a winding-sheet. A very talented writer, whom everyone admired for wildly different reasons.

Setting

The play takes place in Abel's Hill cemetery on Abel's Hill, Martha's Vineyard, in December, near midnight. Abel's Hill is a real place, a spectacularly beautiful, mostly nineteenth century Yankee graveyard; it's way too expensive for any mortal to get a plot in now. Lillian Hellman and Dashiell Hammett are buried there. So is John Belushi, whose tombstone kept getting stolen by fans till Dan Ackroyd put a gigantic boulder on Belushi's grave, too huge for anyone to lift. From the crest of the hill you can see the ocean.

The night is beautiful and very cold.

Everyone has shovels, and several have bottles of various liquors.

They are writers so they love words. Their speech is precise, easy, articulate; they are showing off a little. They are at that stage of drunk, right before sloppy, where you are eloquent, impressing yourself. They are making pronouncements, aware of their wit; this mustn't be pinched, crabbed, dour, effortful. They are having fun on this mad adventure; they relish its drama. Underneath is a very deep grief.

They all really loved Ding.

High atop Abel's Hill, a cemetery on Martha's Vineyard. Just athwart the crest. Tombstones all around. The voice of the playwright is heard on tape, with an accompanying obligato of a typewriter's clattering.

THE VOICE OF THE PLAYWRIGHT

Dramatis personae: seven characters, all playwrights. Biff: *(Biff enters)* scruffy, bisexual, one success, several subsequent failures, cannot stay away from political themes though his analysis is not rigorous. He is overdue; he should be home writing; he should not be here. Happy: *(Happy enters)* his early plays were widely admired, then one big success and he's become a Hollywood writer, TV mostly, rich now, a little bored, but very happy. He plans to go back to writing for the theater someday. Aspera: *(Aspera enters)* writes fierce, splendidly intelligent, challenging plays, frequently with lesbian characters, and cannot get an American theater to produce her for love or money. So she lives in London where she is acclaimed. Ottoline: *(Ottoline enters)* African-American, genuinely great, hugely influential experimentalist whom everyone adores but who is now languishing in relative obscurity and neglect. She is the best writer of the bunch and the least well remunerated. She is an old friend of Flatty: *(Flatty enters)* colossally successful, colossally rich. An easy target for negativity of all kinds, though he is in fact a good writer, hugely prolific. Hautflote: *(Hautflote enters carrying the shrouded body of Ding)* writes beautiful, experimental plays; he has a small, loyal following and little financial success. He was the best friend, and is the executor of the estate of Ding: *(Hautflote places Ding's body on the ground)* a dead playwright wrapped in

a winding-sheet. A very talented writer, whom everyone admired for wildly different reasons.
(Hautflote exits. The other playwrights look about uneasily, and then sit. They have come to bury Ding illegally. It's nearly midnight)
Seven characters are too many for a ten-minute play. It'll be twenty minutes long! Fuck it. One of them is dead and the others can all talk fast.
(Hautflote returns with six shovels)
The play takes place in Abel's Hill cemetery, a spectacularly beautiful, mostly nineteenth century Yankee graveyard; it's way too expensive for any mortal to get a plot in now. On Abel's Hill, Martha's Vineyard, in December, near midnight.

(When the voice is finished, Hautflote goes to a nearby headstone, on the side of which is a light switch. He flicks it on; a full moon appears in the sky.)

HAUTFLOTE

Ah!

(The play begins.)

HAUTFLOTE

Here. We should start digging.

ASPERA

Athwart the crest. Facing the sea. As Ding demanded.

OTTOLINE

Isn't this massively illegal?

FLATTY

Trespass, destruction of private property, destruction of an historical landmark, I shouldn't wonder, conveyance of tissue, i.e., poor Ding, in an advanced state of morbidity, on public transportation—

HAUTFLOTE

He's been *preserved.* He's hazardous to no one's health.
He traveled here in a steamer trunk. The porters helped.

BIFF

(Apostrophizing) O please come to me short sweet simple perfect *idea.* A seed, a plot.

HAUTFLOTE

He's under a deadline.

BIFF

I'm doomed.

HAUTFLOTE

Now shoulder your shovels . . .

BIFF

There's no dignity, have you noticed? In being *this.* An American playwright. What is that?

OTTOLINE

Well, we drink.

HAPPY

No one really drinks now. None of us, at least not publicly.

FLATTY

I can't remember something.

HAPPY

We're . . . *(Looking for the word)*

FLATTY

A name.

HAPPY

Healthier!

HAUTFLOTE

What name?

FLATTY

The name of the country that makes me despair.

HAPPY

But tonight we are drunk.

BIFF

In honor of Ding.

HAUTFLOTE

What letter does it begin with?

BIFF

Poor Ding.

(They all look at Ding. Little pause.)

ASPERA

"And Poor Ding Who Is Dead."

(Little pause. They all look at Ding.)

FLATTY

R.

HAUTFLOTE

Rwanda.

FLATTY

That's it.

OTTOLINE
How could you *forget,* Flatty? Rwanda?

FLATTY
I've never had a head for names. Not in the news much anymore, Rwanda.

OTTOLINE
We are afraid to stick the shovel in.

HAUTFLOTE
Yes.

OTTOLINE
Believing it to be a desecration.

HAUTFLOTE
Of this holy earth.

OTTOLINE
Not *holy*: pure. Authentic.

HAPPY
Yankee.

OTTOLINE
Pilgrim.

HAPPY
Puritan.

OTTOLINE
Forefatherly. Originary.

ASPERA
Oh fuck me, "originary"; John Belushi's buried here!

FLATTY

And he had enough drugs in him when he died to poison all the waters from here to Nantucket.

OTTOLINE

And the people steal his tombstone.

FLATTY

No!

OTTOLINE

Or the hill keeps swallowing it up. It doesn't rest in peace. A pretender, you see.

ASPERA

Lillian Hellman's buried here. She's a playwright.

HAUTFLOTE

Appropriate or no, it's what Ding wanted.

OTTOLINE

And that's another thing. It cost two hundred thirty-seven dollars and fifty cents for a round trip ticket. From New York. This is an *island*. Martha's Vineyard is an *island*! Did Ding *realize* that? One has to *ferry* across. Fucking Ding. Maybe *you all* have money. For ferry passage. I don't have money. I've got no money.

FLATTY

I told you I'd pay for you.

OTTOLINE

Well we all know *you've* got money.

BIFF

O come to me short sweet simple idea!

FLATTY

I want something magical to happen.

BIFF

A plot. The horseleech hath two daughters. It's a start. And these daughters . . . Do . . . What?

HAPPY

They cry!

OTTOLINE

Give, give!

BIFF

Brecht in exile circumnavigated the globe. Berlin. Skovsbostrand. Stockholm. Helsinki. Leningrad. Moscow. Vladivostock. Manila. L.A. Quick stop in D.C. to visit the HUAC. New York. Paris. Zurich. Salzburg. Prague. Berlin. An American playwright, what is that? Never in exile, always in extremis. The list of cities: AIDS, loss, fear of infection, unsafe sex, he says gazing upon the corpse of a fallen comrade. I fuck men and women. I dream my favorite actor has been shot by the police, I dream I shoot Jesse Helms in the head and it doesn't kill him . . .

FLATTY

Eeewww, *politics.*

BIFF

I dream we are intervening in Bosnia merely to give Germany hegemony over Eastern Europe. Why, I dream myself in my dream asking myself, Do you dream that? You do not dream a play, you *write* a play. And this play is due, and there's *(Pointing to Ding's corpse)* the deadline. I write in my notebook that I am glad we are sending troops to former Yugoslavia but I *(He makes the "in quotes" gesture with his fingers)* "inadvertently" spell troops "T-R-O-U-P-E-S" as in troupes as in theatrical troupes, traveling players, we are sending *troupes* to former Yugoslavia.

HAUTFLOTE

I don't think we can avoid it any longer. The digging.

FLATTY

I imagine it's worth serious jail time for us all.

HAPPY

Incarcerated playwrights. Now *that* has dignity. Until it's learned what for.

BIFF

I repulse myself, I am not of this earth, if I were more serious I would be an essayist if I were more observant a novelist more articulate more intelligent a poet more . . . succinct more *ballsy* a screenwriter and then I could buy an apartment.

HAUTFLOTE

Fuck the public. It's all Ding asked for. He never got his own, alive.

ASPERA

Poor poor Ding.

HAUTFLOTE

He grew obsessed with this cemetery, in his final months. We visited it years ago. On a day trip, we could never afford . . . to *stay* here. Or anywhere. Or anything. Health insurance. "Bury me on Abel's Hill." His final words.

I think he thought this place would give him a retroactive pedigree.

OTTOLINE

That's it, *pedigree*, not *holiness*. Blood, genes. Of which we playwrights are envious. We're mutts. Amphibians.

ASPERA

Not of the land nor of the sea. Not of the page nor of the moment.

HAPPY

Perdurable page. Fleeting moment.

FLATTY

Something magical should happen now.

HAUTFLOTE

Ding wanted to belong. Or rather, he never wanted not to. Or rather he never didn't want to, he *wanted* to not want to, but did. In his final months he grew finical.

ASPERA

When I saw him he wasn't finical, he was horrible. He looked horrible and he screamed at everyone all day and all night and there was no way he could get warm, ever. It was quite a change. I hadn't seen him in months, I was visiting from London—WHERE I LIVE, *IN EXILE,* PRODUCED, APPLAUDED, *LAUDED* EVEN and NO ONE IN AMERICA WILL TOUCH MY WORK—but anyway he was somehow very very angry but not bitter. One felt envied, but not blamed. At Ding's deathbed.

HAUTFLOTE

Ding Bat. Der Dingle. Ding-An-Sich.

HAPPY

I remember being impressed when I learned that the HIV virus, which has robbed us of our Ding, reads and writes its genetic alphabets backwards, RNA transcribing DNA transcribing RNA, hence *retro*virus, reverse transcription. I'm not gay but I am a Jew and so of course I, too, "read backwards, write backwards"; I think of Hebrew.

FLATTY

You're not gay?

HAPPY

No.

FLATTY

You're *not*?

HAPPY

No.

FLATTY

Everyone thinks you are. Everyone wants to sleep with you. Everyone. *Everyone.*
Oops.
You were saying?

HAPPY

I was saying that in my grief I thought . . . Well here I attempt a metaphor doomed to fail . . . I mean here we are, playwrights in a graveyard, here to dig, right? So, digging, I think: HIV, reverse transcribing, dust to dust, writing backwards, Hebrew and the Great and Terrible magic of that backwards alphabet, which runs against the grain, counter to the current of European tradition, heritage, thought: a language of fiery, consuming revelation, of refusal, the proper way, so I was taught, to address oneself to God . . . *(He puts his hands on Ding's body)* Perhaps, maybe, this backwards-writing viral nightmare is keeping some secret, subterraneanly affianced to a principle of . . . Reversals: good reversals and also very bad, where good meets bad, perhaps, the place of mystery where back meets

forth, where our sorrow's not the point, where the forward flow of life brutally throws itself into reverse, to reveal . . . *(He lies alongside the body, curls up to it, head on Ding's shoulder, listening)* What? Hebrew always looked to me like zipper teeth unzipped. What awesome thing is it we're zipping open? To what do we return when we write in reverse? What's relinquished, what's released?
What does it sound like I'm doing here?

ASPERA

It sounds like you're equating Hebrew and AIDS.

HAPPY

I'm—

ASPERA

I'm not Jewish but I am a dyke and I think either way, AIDS equals Hebrew or the reverse, you're in BIG trouble. I'm going to beat you up.

HAPPY

Not *equals*, I . . . I'm lonely. I'm among playwrights. Back East for the first time in months. So I get to talk. And none of you listen anyway. In Culver City everyone listens, they listen listen listen. They take notes. They take you at your word. You are playwrights. So be inattentive. If you paid attention you'd be novelists.

FLATTY

Aspera has spent five years in London. She's acquired the listening disease.

OTTOLINE

Soon, unless she watches herself, she will be an American playwright no longer but British, her plays will be all nuance, inference.

FLATTY

Yes, nuance, unless she's careful, or a socialist feminist.

BIFF

Everyone hates you Flatty.

OTTOLINE

Oops.

FLATTY

(Unphased, not missing a beat) And then there will be no nuance at all.

ASPERA

Does everyone hate you?

FLATTY

No, they don't.

ASPERA

I live in London now, I'm out of the loop.

FLATTY

They don't hate me, they envy me my money.

ASPERA

(To Happy) I wouldn't *really* beat you up.

FLATTY

I could buy and sell the lot of you. Even *you* Happy and *you write sitcoms*. There. I've said it. I am wealthy. My plays have made me wealthy. I am richer than essayists, novelists, at least the respectable ones, and all poets ever. Envy is rather *like* hatred but as it's more debilitating to its votaries and votaresses (because it's so inherently undignified) it's of less danger ultimately to its targets.

BIFF

I don't envy your money. I envy your reviews.

HAUTFLOTE

I think we should dig now and bury Ding. This ground is patrolled. The night doesn't last forever. Ding's waiting.

OTTOLINE

(Softly, firmly) Ding's dead.

I love this place. It was worth two hundred and thirty-seven dollars and fifty cents to get here. Yes Flatty you can pay my way. Send me a check. Biff's got a point. It's the reviews, isn't it. I've worked tirelessly for decades. Three at least. What I have done no one has ever done and no one does it nearly so well. But what I do is break the vessels because they never fit me right and I despise their elegance and I like the sound the breaking makes, it's a new music. What I do is make mess apparent or make apparent messes, I cannot tell which myself I signal disenfranchisement, dysfunction, disinheritance well I *am* a black woman what do they expect it's hard stuff but it's life but I am *perverse* I do not want my stories straight up the narrative the narrative the miserable fucking narrative the universe is post-Cartesian post-Einsteinian it's not at any rate what it's *post*-to-be let's throw some curve balls already who cares if they never cross the plate it's hard too hard for folks to apprehend easy so I get no big money reviews and no box office and I'm broke, I'm fifty or sixty or maybe I've turned eighty, I collected the box at the Cafe Cinno yes I am THAT old, and poor but no matter, I have a great talent for poverty. Oblivion, on the other hand, scares me. Death. And this may shock you but *(To Flatty)* I ENVY you . . . your RENOWN. *(Roaring) I DON'T WANT ANOTHER OBIE! I want a hit! I want to hit a home run! I WANT A MARQUEE!* I'm too old to be ashamed of my hunger.

BIFF

O come to me short sweet *(He blows a raspberry)*. There's just no dignity. I am oppressed by theater critics.

FLATTY

I gave up on dignity *years* ago. I am prolific. That's my revenge. If you want dignity you should marry a lighting designer.

OTTOLINE

Perhaps now we have worn out our terror, or at least winded it.

HAUTFLOTE

At darkest midnight December in the bleak midwinter athwart the crest of Abel's Hill on Martha's Vineyard six moderately inebriated playwrights stood shovels poised to inter—

FLATTY

Illegally.

HAUTFLOTE

. . . the earthly remains of a seventh.

HAPPY

Who might at least have agreed to the convenience of a cremation.

HAUTFLOTE

Being a creature of paper as well as of the fleeting moment Ding naturally had a horror of fire. *I knew him best.* For a long time now. I loved him.

OTTOLINE

We all did.

HAUTFLOTE

Yet not one of us dares break ground.

HAPPY

Wind perhaps, but never ground.

ASPERA

Wind for sure but not the Law. But is it the Law or what's underground which immobilizes us? Incarceration or an excess of freedom? Enchainment or liberation? For who knows what dreams may come? Who knows what's underneath? Who knows if anything is, if the shovel will strike stone, or pay dirt, or nothing whatsoever?

BIFF

It's the Nothing stopping me. I can speak only for myself.

FLATTY

Bad thing in a playwright.

BIFF

The horseleech hath two daughters. There's a play in there, somewhere, of course. I used to say: it won't come out. Fecal or something, expulsive metaphor. I was stuffed, full and withholding. In more generous times. Before the fear . . . of the Deficit, before the Balanced Budget became the final face of the Angel of the Apocalypse. Now instead I say: I'm not going to go there. A geographical metaphor. Why? *I'm nearly forty* is one explanation. *"There"* meaning . . . That bleachy bone land. Into that pit. That plot. To meet that deadline.

OTTOLINE

The play is due . . . ?

BIFF

Day after yesterday.

HAPPY

Rehearsals starting . . . ?

BIFF

Start*ed.*

ASPERA

What, without a script?

BIFF

They're *improvising.*

(Everyone shudders.)

FLATTY

You shouldn't be here! You should be home writing!

BIFF

Did I mention how much I hate you, Flatty.

FLATTY

Marry a lighting designer. It worked for me. Sobered me right up.

HAPPY

I never meant . . . This reverse transcription thing. I'll work on it.

ASPERA

You do that.

HAPPY

I never meant to equate Hebrew and . . . It's just the words: reverse transcription. *Thinking* about it. Something I can't help doing. Writing began with the effort to record speech. All writing is an attempt to fix intangibles—thought, speech, what the eye observes—fixed on clay tablets, in stone, on paper. Writers *capture*. We playwrights on the other hand write or rather "wright" to set these free again. Not inscribing, not *de*-scribing but . . . *ex*-scribing (?) . . . "W-R-I-G-H-T," that archaism, because it's something earlier we do, cruder, something one does with one's mitts, one's paws. To claw words up . . . !

(Happy falls to his knees besides Ding, and starts to dig with his hands.)

HAPPY

To startle words back into the air again, to . . . evanesce. It is . . . unwriting, to do it is to die, yes, but. A lively form of doom.

ASPERA

Ah, so now you are equating . . .

HAPPY

It's not about *equation.* It's about the transmutation of horror into meaning.

ASPERA

Doomed to fail.

HAPPY

Dirty work . . . *(He shows his hands)*

ASPERA

A mongrel business. This Un-earthing.

HAUTFLOTE

For which we Un-earthly are singularly fit. Now or never.

BIFF

I'm nearly forty. My back hurts.

FLATTY

Whose doesn't? No dignity but in our labors.

(They hoist their shovels.)

ASPERA

Good night old Ding. Rest easy baby. And flights of self-dramatizing hypochondriacal hypersensitive self-pitying paroxysmical angels saddlebag you off to sleep.

BIFF

(Apostrophizing Ding's corpse) Oh Dog Weary.

HAUTFLOTE

Many of these graves are cenotaphs, you know, empty tombs, honorifics. Sailors lost on whalers, lost at sea, no body ever found, air and memory interred instead. All other headstones in the graveyard peristalithic to these few empty tombs, whose ghostly drama utterly overwhelms The Real.

(Hautflote waves his hand in the air, a downbeat. Ella Fitzgerald sings "Begin the Beguine.")

OTTOLINE

Dig. Shovel tips to earth.

(They are.)

OTTOLINE

The smell of earth will rise to meet us. Our nostrils fill with dark brown, roots' ends, decomposing warmth and manufactory, earthworm action. The loam.

FLATTY

I don't want to go to jail. Doesn't David Mamet live around here somewhere?

OTTOLINE

Push in.

(They do.)

THE END

Hydriotaphia

OR

The Death of Dr. Browne

An Epic Farce about Death and Primitive Capital Accumulation

This play is dedicated
to the memory of
Dr. Max Deutscher
1915–1980
scar-tough & skinless,
wrathful & wonderful . . .

Production History

Hydriotaphia or The Death of Doctor Browne received its first production in June 1987 at HOME for Contemporary Theater and Art in New York City. It was produced by Heat & Light Co., Inc. It was directed by the author and assisted directed by Michael Mayer. Lights were designed by Steven Rosen, costumes were by Priscilla Stampa, sets were by committee and exigency and Lesley Kushner. The music was by Mel Marvin. And the cast was as follows:

SIR THOMAS BROWNE	Stephen Spinella
HIS SOUL	Maria Makis
DAME DOROTHY BROWNE	Roberta Levine
BABBO	Priscilla Stampa
MACCABEE	Peter Guttmacher
DR. EMIL SCHADENFREUDE	Ümit Celebi
DR. LEVITICUS DOGWATER	Lee Grober
LEONARD PUMPKIN	Tim White
THE ABBESS OF X	Alexandra Rambusch
DOÑA ESTRELITA	Carmalita Fuentes
SARAH	Cheryl Thornton
MARY	Kimberly T. Flynn
RUTH	Camryn Manheim
DEATH	Sam Calandrino

Hydriotaphia or The Death of Doctor Browne was produced by the Graduate Acting Program of NYU's Tisch School of the Arts in April 1997. The director was Michael Wilson; sets were designed by Michael Lapthorn, costumes were by Theresa Squire, the lighting design was by Lap-Chi Chu, sound design was by Darron L. West, the composer was Mel Marvin and the stage manager was Stacy P. Hughes. The cast was as follows:

SIR THOMAS BROWNE	Jason Butler Harner
HIS SOUL	Jeff Whitty
DAME DOROTHY BROWNE	Anita Dashiell
BABBO	Angel Desai
MACCABEE	Christian Lincoln
DR. EMIL SCHADENFREUDE	Matthew Miller
DR. LEVITICUS DOGWATER	Sam Catlin
LEONARD PUMPKIN	Tom Butler
THE ABBESS OF X	Michael Hyatt
DOÑA ESTRELITA	Teri Lamm
SARAH	Christina Apathy
MARY	Dionne Lea
RUTH	Christopher Kelly
DEATH	John Eddins

In 1998, *Hydriotaphia or The Death of Dr. Browne* received a co-production by the Alley Theatre in Houston, Texas (Gregory Boyd, Artistic Director; Paul R. Tetreault, Managing Director), and Berkeley Repertory Theatre in California (Tony Taccone, Artistic Director; Susan Medak, Managing Director). In April of that year the play opened at the Alley with Michael Wilson as director; Jeff Cowie was scenic and projection designer, David C. Woolard was costume designer, Michael Lincoln was the lighting designer, Joe Pino was sound designer, original music was composed by Mel Marvin and the stage manager was Kristin Fox. The cast was as follows:

SIR THOMAS BROWNE	Jonathan Hadary
HIS SOUL	Jenny Bacon
DAME DOROTHY BROWNE	Shelley Williams
BABBO	Bettye Fitzpatrick
MACCABEE	Alex Allen Morris
DR. EMIL SCHADENFREUDE	John Feltch
DR. LEVITICUS DOGWATER	Charles Dean
LEONARD PUMPKIN	Kyle Fabel
THE ABBESS OF X	Sharon Lockwood
DOÑA ESTRELITA	Annalee Jefferies
SARAH	Delia MacDougall
MARY	Moya Furlow
RUTH	Louise Chegwidden
DEATH	Paul Hope

In September 1998 the production moved to Berkeley Repertory Theatre (Tony Taccone, Artistic Director; Susan Medak, Managing Director). Michael Wilson was production supervisor, Ethan McSweeny was the director. Scenic and projection designer was Jeff Cowie, costumes were by David C. Woolard, lighting design was by Peter Maradudin, sound design was by Matthew Spiro, original music was composed by Mel Marvin, the production stage manager was Michael Suenkel and the stage manager was Juliet N. Pokorny. The cast was as follows:

SIR THOMAS BROWNE	Jonathan Hadary
HIS SOUL	Anika Noni Rose
DAME DOROTHY BROWNE	Shelley Williams
BABBO	Sloane Shelton
MACCABEE	Rod Gnapp
DR. EMIL SCHADENFREUDE	Charles Dean
DR. LEVITICUS DOGWATER	J. R. Horne
LEONARD PUMPKIN	Hamish Linklater
THE ABBESS OF X	Sharon Lockwood
DOÑA ESTRELITA	Wilma Bonet
SARAH	Delia MacDougall
MARY	Moya Furlow
RUTH	Louise Chegwidden
DEATH	Paul Hope

Thanks to Michael Mayer for waking the play from its long sleep, and to Zelda Fichandler for approving its first production in eleven years. Michael Wilson got it back on its feet and found its soul again. The NYU cast was magnificent, the Berkeley Rep cast was beyond heroic; the original cast performs the play nightly in my heart of hearts. I am very grateful to Stephen Spinella, Jason Butler Harner and Jonathan Hadary, my three Brownes, for their glorious incarnations of the nasty bloated logorrheic old bugger. The staff at Berkeley Rep saved my life, and are the Platonic ideal of a theater staff. Amy Potozkin and Susie Medak graciously endured a lot of anxious phumphing from me, and Michael Suenkel, the stage manager, made the impossible seem a routine matter of little regard.

More than anyone else, my deepest thanks, and much love, go to Tony Taccone, who has been over the years a great friend, in every regard a true gentleman of the theater, and a rare hand with a rubber chicken.

Sir Thomas Browne and the Restoration

The number of the dead long exceedeth all that shall live. The night of time far surpasseth the day, and who knows when was the Aequinox? Every houre addes unto that current Arithmetique, which scarce stands one moment. And since death must be the *Lucina* of life, and even Pagans could doubt whether thus to live, were to dye. Since our longest Sunne sets at right decensions, and makes but winter arches, and therefore it cannot be long before we lie down in darkness, and have our light in ashes. Since the brother of death daily haunts us with dying *memento's*, and time that grows old it self, bids us hope no long duration: Diuturnity is a dream and a folly of expectation.

Darknesse and light divide the course of time, and oblivion shares with memory a great part even of our living beings; we slightly remember our felicities, and the smartest stroaks of affliction leave but short smart upon us. Sense endureth no extremities, and sorrows destroy us or themselves. To weep into stones are fables. Afflictions induce callosities, miseries are slippery, or fall like snow upon us, which notwithstanding is no unhappy stupidity. To be ignorant of evils to come, and forgetfull of evils past, is a mercifull provision in nature, whereby we digest the mixture of our few and evil dayes, and our delivered senses not lapsing into cutting remembrances, our sorrows are not kept raw by the edge of repetitions.

[from "Hydriotaphia or Urne-Buriall"
—SIR THOMAS BROWNE

SIR THOMAS BROWNE (1605–1682) was a writer of prodigious genius, coiner of an English-language prose style of such voluptuous baroquosity it melts the straight lines and right angles of the Euclidean universe, stretches every assumption of Cartesian logic, and achieves, by means of a remorselessly tortured syntax, something dialectically poised between Rigorous Reason and Ecstatic Delirium; aiming at science and philosophy, his essays achieve vision and poetry instead. Browne's style influenced writers from De Quincey to Melville, and I believe his ornate jeweled swooniness can be discerned as influence in the works of such contemporaries as Michael Ondaatje and Edmund White.

Browne may have been a thoroughly lovely human being; this play is not intended as a portrait of the historical man, any more than it is an accurate portrait of late-mid-seventeenth-century England. If anything, this is a play about the treachery of words, about writing—probably it's better that I let *you* decide what it's about.

Primitive capital accumulation is a term of Karl Marx's and Friedrich Engels's, making reference to the ugly and vital process whereby a nation that is entering the capitalist phase of economic and social relations dislocates its rural populations in the course of a violent land grab by aristocratic and entrepreneurial classes intent on accumulating, by any means necessary, the material resources that provide the bases for mercantile, manufacturing and speculatory fortunes. From the devastation consequent upon such officially sanctioned piracy, an impoverished urban and factory workforce emerges, desperate for wages. Primitive capital accumulation is the nakedly brutal manner in which money was grubbed from people and land, before the camouflaging, cosmeticization, banalization and normalization of such mayhem, before we learned new words for it, like Modernization, Progress, Industrialization—before the invention of Spin.

Shakespeare lived through the tail end of the roughest phase of primitive accumulation in England, and his plays reflect the chaos of the time, their bloodiness, their immense excitement, and the irreconcilable dissonance between Christianity and capitalism, between unstoppered material appetite and Christ's asceticism, His antipathy toward wealth and usury, His preference for the poor. Widespread misery was occasioned by the seizure of common lands, moors and forests, and their transformation into private property. This misery manifested itself chiefly in waves of homeless rural poor descending on the cities, seeking food, shelter, work, and finding less than they needed; in the fiery growth of religious dissidence, religious radicalism and factionalism, challenging the orthodoxy, feeding rivers of ancient class resentment and the explosive pressures generated by a rapidly rising mercantile class rubbing up against a truculent, greedy aristocracy. A social, political revolution in England in the seventeenth century was inevitable.

From 1642–1649, England fought two civil wars, ending with the beheading of the disastrous king Charles I and the establishment of a wobbly Parliamentary republic. In 1653 Oliver Cromwell, a personage of spectacular contradictions, noble intentions and a pronounced capacity for barbarism, backed by the army, ascended to an uneasy dictatorship as Lord Protector and Head of State. In 1658 Cromwell died of malaria, and all hope for a real republic ended quickly; in 1660, with the backing of part of the army, the monarchy was restored in the person of Charles II, who one year later dug up Cromwell's grave in Westminster Abbey, hung his corpse in Tyburn and then decapitated it, keeping the head on a pike atop Westminster Hall where it remained till Charles II died.

Sir Thomas Browne lived through this period, a steadfast supporter of the monarchy throughout the civil wars, the Commonwealth and the Protectorate, for which loyalty he was rewarded with a knighthood in 1671. *Hydriotaphia* takes place in an obviously askew version of this postrevolutionary England, after the Restoration of the Old Order Transformed.

In 1664 Browne's testimony, consisting of disinterested theological speculation, helped hang two women accused of witchcraft.

Dramatis Personae

SIR THOMAS BROWNE, a physician and author. He's fifty years old. He is a thin man, but his body is hugely swollen. He is very wealthy and he is dying.

HIS SOUL, tiny, beautiful, but a little soiled; it lives behind the headboard of Browne's deathbed. It sings beautifully.

DAME DOROTHY BROWNE, Sir Thomas's wife, forty or forty-five; she's had fourteen children and a very hard life. She is dressed simply but elegantly.

BABBO, Browne's nanny when he was a child, and now his cook. She is very old but busy as a little steam engine—not frail, her brain a little dim, and sweet. She chews a stick of cinnamon.

MACCABBEE, Browne's amanuensis/servant/laboratory assistant. Maccabbee has the clap and it has eaten away his nose. In his nose's place he wears a brass prophylaxis, like Tycho Brahe did. The brass nose is held in place with ribbon tied around his head.

DR. EMIL SCHADENFREUDE, Browne's physician, a Hessian doctor living in Norfolk. He speaks with a remarkable German accent. He is dressed in High Restoration style, as if eager to blend in with London society. A pleasant man enjoying life and his work, an enthusiast.

DR. LEVITICUS DOGWATER, Browne's pastor and his business partner. A Protestant cleric, he dresses elegantly but severely. He is very robust, and he speaks with a stutter.

LEONARD PUMPKIN, the local gravedigger. He is very handsome and very poor, about twenty-five years old. His hands are always filthy filthy filthy.

THE ABBESS OF X, née Alice Browne, Sir Thomas's sister, presumed drowned but actually living as the Mother Superior of a convent of British ex-pat assassin nuns. She is dressed in a *very* severe and *very* elegant (but suitable for action) nun's habit.

DOÑA ESTRELITA, the wife of the Spanish ambassador to the British court, a former lover of Browne's. She is fifty, immensely wealthy and, when not in disguise, her couture is the very zenith of European decadence and beauty. She speaks with a magnificent Spanish accent.

SARAH, a ranter woman, homeless, lives in the forest, a witch. She is dressed in rags. Probably in her twenties or thirties, though so begrimed and worn by life it's hard to tell. She is a person of tremendous power.

MARY, a ranter, just like Sarah, but of a more thoughtful and gentle disposition.

RUTH, a ranter, more bellicose than the other two, and the best at ranting.

DEATH, an immensely fat man, green skin, skull showing through scalp, dressed in rotting Stuart-era finery, wrapped, like Marley's ghost, in chains from which dangle ledger books and counting boxes. He resembles a wealthy silk merchant. He is nearly seven feet tall, terrifying to behold and he loves to eat.

Setting

Norfolk, England (sort of)
April 3, 1667 (more or less)

Some Thoughts about the Play:

It is very long. Do it fast. This is a rough, aggressive age.

It is very long. Do it fast, but make it real. It lives only if it addresses and presents relationships between real (and unreal) people with real, immense needs, and fears and hopes. Played rapidly without specificity and intelligence it will feel to the audience a million years long.

It is very long because it is full of words; it is, in fact, very much a play about words and writing. The words are not hurdles to leap across and over on your way to some big juicy inarticulate emotion, you American actors! The scenes full of words are not inaccurate and unreliable suggestions for some potential event to which the play alludes elliptically but does not actually describe, you American directors! The scenes must be read and analyzed carefully and precisely (specifically) and imaginatively (but groundedly) with an eye toward *objectives* and *needs* and *plausible psychological development*. The characters live and do what they come onstage to do (and they *always always* come onstage to *do* something) through their words.

Frequent address of the audience is fine; more than fine, it's important. The main relationships are between the characters but the audience ought to be included when possible and not injurious to the life of the relationships onstage.

As for Dr. Browne, his entire inner life, which is almost entirely articulated *(see play's Afterword)*, is shared directly with the audience. The audience, for him, *is* his inner life, or at least that to which his inner life is spoken.

The Set

Central should be Browne's deathbed, with a high marble headboard like a tombstone. The room should be richly appointed and cluttered with books, scrolls, astrolabes, telescopes, microscopes, models of engines, a model of the quarry, models of buildings, sacks of gold, musical instruments, anatomical charts, skulls of various animals including many human skulls, bottles of medicine, bottles with dead things and necrotic tissues floating inside, paintings (including several portraits of Browne), surveying equipment, nautical equipment, daggers and swords and harquebuses, abacuses—and a cobwebbed, long-unused writing desk with split pens, dried ink in dusty inkwells and great sheaves and stacks of paper, endlessly scribbled upon.

There is a plinth, empty, awaiting the arrival of the urn. When it arrives, the urn should be astonishing, blackened ancient terra-cotta with bas-relief faces in ghastly rictuses and agonies of death—coins on their eyes, tongues distended, jaws either rigor-mortised opened or clamped shut with mortuary bandage. It should be very sinister and old. It will be required to cough up a delicate spume of dust *and* belch forth a thick cloud of smoke. Smoke is smoke and dust is dust and a spume is different from a cloud and yes the urn must be able to do both of those things.

Music

His Soul's songs have been set to beautiful music by Mel Marvin (permission for use may be obtained through the Joyce Ketay Agency).

"There Is a Land of Pure Delight" is a traditional English hymn, and can be found in hymnals. The melody is traditional. The words are by Isaac Watts. It should be sung in four-part harmony.

Costumes

The costumes should be sumptuous and extravagant; neither leadenly historically accurate nor too silly! There should probably be a touch (only a touch) of the modern about the look of the characters, for instance, period clothing but no wigs. Remember that these people live in the country so wigs and other Restoration geegaws are probably not appropriate.

Browne's swollen body and Sarah's naked body in Scene Four should be achieved by anatomically articulated, over-the-top body stockings (genitals included). Real nudity is too . . . real.

The Accents

This is the way I described the accent issue in the first drafts:

> The aristocrats all speak standard American English, crisp and clear.
>
> The bumpkins speak a made-up dialect. Simply pronounce the words exactly as they are written—it will sound a little like Brooklynese, though it should not be done with a Brooklyn accent; its vocabulary is derived from Yorkshire, Brooklyn, and also *Krazy Kat* (the comic strip; not the cartoon). *It is not southern American, Texan, Irish or African-American!!* You will get it right if you just read it out loud as it is spelled, *without accent of any kind.* They speak rapidly and clearly. To be understood by the audience you have to speak very very clearly. Schadenfreude's accent should be a great trilled and guttural German. (*Please*, actor playing Schadenfreude, do *not* substitute "sh" for "s"—be intelligible and crisp.) Estrelita's accent should be a great, rich, voluptuous Spanish.

(Actor playing Estrelita, do *not* add an "e" to every word beginning with "s," and do not do a Castilian lisp.)

Dogwater's stutter, again, should be exactly as written—*please*, the actor playing him should *not* make up his own stutters, or add to the ones written. Dogwater has great control over his impediment and has the lightness and crispness that implies. Remember, he speaks for a living! Adding and improvising stuttering will kill the jokes and make the speeches interminable and unintelligible.

I would add to the above that it now seems to me *possible* that the whole thing could be done with British accents, the peasant dialect probably a Midlands dialect—though if this option is tried, the made-up peasant words wouldn't change, just the accent. I like the American sound but perhaps a British sound would work.

Because of the strangeness of the peasant language, regardless of which side of the Atlantic, accentually speaking, your production winds up on, you should play the first scenes with a special precision and care. Babbo and Maccabbee's first speeches will tend to affright audiences with their linguistic alienness, and must serve as an accessible, comprehensible template for listening to the play.

I hope Dogwater's stutter is not offensive to anyone with a stutter—several people with stutters have seen the play and have not taken offense, but using a disability in a comedy always raises complex questions. And Dogwater is a comic character—the audience should laugh at him, though not because he stutters. His stutter is another kind of eloquence, he is in magnificent control of it, unapologetic, though vulnerable, as we see at the end of Scene Two, to mockery. As I mentioned, this is a play about language and words, and I think the accents, made-up words, Dogwater's stutter and everyone's loquacity are all part of a general reveling in language and in the ways language is used.

Intermissions

There must be two intermissions, one after Act Two, one after Act Three. This means that the middle section is short; that's fine. Putting the second intermission after Act Four is a bad idea; having only one intermission is worse.

Act One

CONTEMPTUS MUNDI

Bright Fresh Early April Morning

The sickroom. The deathbed. Dr. Browne lying in it, covered, rattling feebly, asleep. The curtains are drawn and it is dark. At the foot of the bed, on the floor, Maccabbee and Babbo are fucking.

MACCABBEE AND BABBO

HUH HUH HUH HUH HUH HUH *HUH*!

BABBO

(Sharply) Sssshhh!

(They both sit up, look at the bed, see Dr. Browne breathing, and go back to their copulation.)

MACCABBEE AND BABBO

HUH! HUH! HUH! HUH! HUH! HUH HUUUUUUUUUHHHH!!!!

(Babbo sticks her legs straight up in the air and her slippers fly over her head across the room. They have finished.)

MACCABBEE

(Fastening his pants) Ouf.

BABBO

Shame.

MACCABBEE

'Tis natchural.

BABBO

Verra. But it still bin a shame. We shouldn't oughta a done dat. In here. Him dying onna bed 'n' you with da clap so bad yer nose is rot off.

MACCABBEE

Gets me going, da smella da room.

BABBO

Dat's disgusting.

MACCABBEE

I predick dat he takes his last breaf before noon. Ef he don't pop first. Dat's my scientific summestimation.

BABBO

Poor Dr. Browne. So swole . . .

MACCABBEE

Think a all dem juices.

(They look at each other, a lascivious look.)

MACCABBEE

You wanna?

(As they begin to embrace again, Dr. Browne sits up suddenly, makes an abrupt horrible noise, falls back and begins to spasm and gurgle.)

BABBO

Ah Christ! We gone and disrespected him to da portals a death!

MACCABBEE

Go get da missus.

BABBO

(Shrieking) Aaaaahhh!!!

MACCABBEE

Da Event! 'Tis imminent! Scoot, 'n' hurry!

(Babbo runs out one door, Maccabbee the other.
There is a simultaneous darkening and a build of strange, gray light. Music. Above the headboard a white ladder descends, just the tip, a light comes down from Heaven, and His Soul strains upward, trying to reach the ladder; meanwhile Death, growling, enters the room and approaches the bed. Death lays a chilly hand on Dr. Browne's throat and from the sleeve of his cloak he draws a huge carving knife.)

DEATH

At . . . last . . . I've . . . waited . . . so long . . . for you . . . THOMAS . . . come . . . I am ravenous . . . how I love—

(Death raises the knife.)

DR. BROWNE

(Sitting up, eyes still shut, fierce) NOT YET, GODDAMNIT!

(The lights revert abruptly to normal, the music dies as though running out of batteries, Death growls in frustration and runs out the door; His Soul gives up reaching for the ladder and drops down behind the headboard.)

HIS SOUL

Shit.

(The light from Heaven dies. Dr. Browne opens his eyes, shivers with cold, wide awake into terror.)

DR. BROWNE

Maccabbee!

(Maccabbee enters.)

MACCABBEE

Yup.

DR. BROWNE

What's the date?

MACCABBEE

Thursday.

DR. BROWNE

The *date*, you idiot.

MACCABBEE

April Three.

DR. BROWNE

My Birthday.

MACCABBEE

No need ta call me a idiot.

DR. BROWNE

My Birthday.

MACCABBEE

'N' many happy returns a da day.

DR. BROWNE

I will die today.

MACCABBEE

I said dat ta Babbo not five minutes gone. I predicket it. From da gurgle 'n' da gasp. 'Tis scientific.

DR. BROWNE

I have trained you well. Fetch the gravedigger. It's morning?

MACCABBEE

Only just.

DR. BROWNE

(Lying back in bed) Go.

(Maccabbee runs out. His Soul sticks its head up, rattles its chains.)

HIS SOUL

Soon! Soon!

DR. BROWNE

Very soon.

HIS SOUL

You stink like a sewer! I can't bear this much longer.

DR. BROWNE

(Straining) I can't release . . . it won't come out . . . *(He gives up)*

(Dame Dorothy Browne hurries in. His Soul disappears.)

DAME DOROTHY

Are you . . . ? Thank God.

DR. BROWNE

Not yet. But soon . . .

(Dame Dorothy goes to windows, pulls open the big drapes. Morning light streams in.)

DAME DOROTHY

Happy Birthday, Thomas. Did you pass a stool? *(Silence. She checks the bedpan. Empty)* Guess not.

DR. BROWNE

I've swollen again.

DAME DOROTHY

You can't have swollen, you haven't eaten in a week.

(Babbo rushes in.)

BABBO

Bin dead?
(She sees him)
Ahhh, thank God. Many happy returns, Dr. Browne. You look spectacala.

DR. BROWNE

I bloat.

BABBO

Mrs. Browne, dose wimmin you let in last night, dey be making a harful warrick in da kitchen, be scarfin down da rah heggs 'n' sucking seeds outa da squash, 'n' one bin slavverin every dropta wine inna pantry. Fer breakfast.

DAME DOROTHY

I have to go now, Thomas. Thomas?

DR. BROWNE

I want to see the gravedigger.

DAME DOROTHY

You don't need a gravedigger.

DR. BROWNE

I have instructions—

BABBO

'N' dey keept it up in halfta nour don't be nuffin potable ner comastible in da place, 'n' no food fer Dr. Browne's funeral.

DAME DOROTHY

Babbo!

BABBO

'N' you better come now 'cause I can't congle with 'em, 'n' twas your idea to let 'em in.

DR. BROWNE

GRAVEDIGGER!

DAME DOROTHY

Babbo, stay here and watch till Dr. Schadenfreude comes. *(She goes)*

DR. BROWNE

I shouldn't scream. It brings on the bloating.

BABBO

Fer aftah da funeral, I thought maybe ta serve plum tart with lemmin grind. It's yer favorite. How'd dat be, Dr. Browne?

DR. BROWNE

I don't care . . . what you serve. I won't be there.

BABBO

Dat's true. But all same, 'tis yer funeral. 'N' you was always such a fussy 'n' patricula man.

DR. BROWNE

Last night
I dreamt I breathed
my final breath, and as I did
my soul
escaped,
rose out of me
like a fat, pale moon.
It floated to the ceiling.
It caught there
in the blackened roof beams,
and stuck. My dead eyes,
my dead eyes saw it wriggle like a fly,
trapped, not
able
to rise any higher.

(His Soul rattles its chains.)

BABBO

(Softly) I think I'll make da tart. Dere bin early plums, so it be tarter dan usual, make everyone pucker 'n' deir eyes water like dey was crying fer you.

(She laughs a little.)

DR. BROWNE

A good plan. There should be tears.

BABBO

I'll weep fer you, Sir Thomas.

DR. BROWNE

Listen, old lady.

BABBO

Listet to what?

DR. BROWNE

That pounding. In the distance. Rolling over the meadows. Boooomm. Boooommm. It's the sound of the engines in the quarry, digging deep.
My engines.
I don't want to die.

(Maccabbee and the gravedigger, Leonard Pumpkin, enter.)

MACCABBEE

Da gravedigger.

(Dr. Schadenfreude enters.)

MACCABBEE

'N' da doctah.

DR. BROWNE

It's my birthday.

DR. SCHADENFREUDE

Congratulations. You look . . . appallingly bad. Your color—it's positively inorganic.

DR. BROWNE

The leeches.

DR. SCHADENFREUDE

In a minute. First—

DR. BROWNE

What?

DR. SCHADENFREUDE

A mercury enema!

DR. BROWNE

NO!

(Dr. Schadenfreude pulls from his bag a frightful gadget, a large glass bottle filled with quicksilver, on one end a syringe plunger, on the other end large phallic-shaped leather nozzle.)

DR. SCHADENFREUDE

Yes.

DR. BROWNE

I refuse.

DR. SCHADENFREUDE

I'm your doctor.

DR. BROWNE

I'll be dead soon. The leeches.

DR. SCHADENFREUDE

Patience. First the enema. We have to try to remove that blockage. Ladies leave.

(Babbo goes. Dr. Schadenfreude notices the gravedigger.)

DR. SCHADENFREUDE

Who are you?

PUMPKIN

Gravedigger.

DR. SCHADENFREUDE

How convenient. Now then.

(Schadenfreude leaps onto the bed with the equipment. He pulls the sheets over his head, which mercifully obscures from our sight the procedure. There is much struggling.)

MACCABBEE

(To Pumpkin) He's gotta tumor. Inna bowels. Like a onion, dey say. Plug him up.

PUMPKIN

A onion?

MACCABBEE

Inna bowels.

PUMPKIN

Gawd.

(Dr. Schadenfreude is finished.)

DR. SCHADENFREUDE

No good. Gunpowder couldn't budge it. Let's bleed him a little.

DR. BROWNE

(Weakly) Leeches . . .

DR. SCHADENFREUDE

Yes, but first we skim off the bad blood, so the leeches don't get sick when they suck. You're a regular sack of toxins, Thomas.

(Schadenfreude takes out a horrible-looking device, like a sap-spigot for syrup gathering; he rams it in Dr. Browne's side, and holds a bucket underneath it to catch the blood, which is running out at an alarming rate.)

DR. BROWNE

I'm . . . so . . . cold . . . no . . . more . . .

(The lights change. Music. His Soul sits up, looking eager. Schadenfreude, Maccabbee and Pumpkin can't see this. Dr. Schadenfreude pulls out the spigot, applies a wad of cotton to the puncture.)

DR. SCHADENFREUDE

Enough for now.

(The lights go back to normal.)

HIS SOUL

(Disappearing) DAMN!

DR. SCHADENFREUDE

And already your color's improving! The wonders of the modern age. Fifty years ago these techniques were unknown. And now the leeches!
Thomas?
Sir Thomas?

(Dr. Browne is unconscious. Dr. Schadenfreude slaps him gently.)

DR. SCHADENFREUDE

Peacefully resting. No leeches for today . . . Well maybe just one.
(He applies a disgusting leech)
Smack smack smack. Little crescent kisses.
(To Pumpkin, who has moved away) Squeamish?

PUMPKIN

Nope.

DR. SCHADENFREUDE

Hard to be squeamish and work in your field. Why don't I know you?

PUMPKIN

New to these parts.

DR. SCHADENFREUDE

Name?

PUMPKIN

Pumpkin.

DR. SCHADENFREUDE

Christian name?

PUMPKIN

Leonard.

DR. SCHADENFREUDE

What happened to the old gravedigger?

PUMPKIN

Died.

DR. SCHADENFREUDE

Your predecessor and I had an agreement. I pay crown sterling for reasonably intact cadavers. Dr. Schadenfreude.

(He proffers his hand. Pumpkin shakes it. Schadenfreude wipes it with a hankie.)

DR. SCHADENFREUDE

Medical research. Highly scientific work. Right, Maccabbee?

MACCABBEE

Oh, yoop.

DR. SCHADENFREUDE

How are Browne's experiments coming along?

MACCABBEE

Well, Doctah Browne mostly loss interest inna lass few weeks, oncet da swelling incepted. We was doing a experiment ta see if da dogs would eat rotted birds.

DR. SCHADENFREUDE

Did they?

MACCABBEE

O sure dey bin chompet on stuff so rotted da flies wouldn't go near it.

DR. SCHADENFREUDE

From which you conclude . . .

MACCABBEE

Da conclusions was fer Sir Thomas ta extrapolate 'n' send to da Royal Academy in London. I mostly took care a da nasty stuff. But I guess . . . I conclude . . . dat dogs . . . like rotted meat.

DR. SCHADENFREUDE

And *thrive* from eating it.

MACCABBEE

Yah, dey do at dat. 'Tis nauseating.

DR. SCHADENFREUDE

From which we may conclude, perhaps, that there is a vitality in putrefaction, a life in death: rats born in sacks of mouldy grain, maggots blossoming in rancid meat, bustle bugs in the water-tap scumbeard—

MACCABBEE

Science bin amazement!

DR. SCHADENFREUDE

Browne's last Will and Testament. Is it available for viewing?

MACCABBEE

Han't heard nuffin about it.

DR. SCHADENFREUDE

(Flipping Maccabbee a coin) If you happen to hear that he's specified the name of his eulogist, fill me in. I'm certain I'll be asked to eulogize him. I knew him inside and out! Everyone says he was a genius. They say the king himself might attend . . .
(To Pumpkin) Mendicants, vagrants, charity corpses—as long as they're reasonably fresh.

(Dr. Schadenfreude starts out as Dame Dorothy enters.)

DR. SCHADENFREUDE

(Bowing) Dame Dorothy.

DAME DOROTHY

It's his birthday. He says he'll die today.

DR. SCHADENFREUDE

Cradle to crypt, a mark of character. The Romans did it.

DAME DOROTHY

By killing themselves.

DR. SCHADENFREUDE

Better a warm bath and a sharp knife than a slow, wasting death. Your husband I'm sure would agree with me. If he was conscious.
Madame. *(Bows and goes)*

DAME DOROTHY

Maccabbee, show him out.

MACCABBEE

(Gesturing for Pumpkin to leave) Dis way, Pumpkin.

DAME DOROTHY

No, not him. He can stay for a moment. Show the doctor out.

MACCABBEE

Da doctah's been here every day fer a month. He knows how ta get out.

DAME DOROTHY

Well, just in case.

MACCABBEE

In case what?

DAME DOROTHY

Maccabbee, go!

MACCABBEE

(Pointing to Pumpkin) How come he getsa stay?

DAME DOROTHY

I want to discuss the sarcophagus.

MACCABBEE

Da what?

(Dame Dorothy points to the door and glowers. Maccabbee grudgingly exits.)

DAME DOROTHY

Leonard.

PUMPKIN

Dorfy.

DAME DOROTHY

Wait.

(Dame Dorothy tiptoes to Dr. Browne, assures herself that he is unconscious, checks the door and windows, then goes to Pumpkin and kisses him passionately.)

PUMPKIN

(Pulling away) DORFY!

DAME DOROTHY

He's sleeping.

PUMPKIN

'Tis perverse.

DAME DOROTHY

I know. I haven't seen you since Monday evening.

PUMPKIN

Busy week. Dropping like—

DAME DOROTHY

(Throatily) Come here. Leonard . . .

PUMPKIN

I mean, look at him. Poor ole balloon.

DAME DOROTHY

I don't want to look at him.

PUMPKIN

Let's go to da woods.

DAME DOROTHY

(Pulling him down to the rug) I can't leave. My place is here, with my husband.

PUMPKIN

Ent you sad he bin dying?

DAME DOROTHY

Grief . . . is a highly personal thing. It's spring, Leonard. I've been cold a long time. Your hands are so strong and so filthy.

PUMPKIN

Grave dirt.

DAME DOROTHY

Poor Pumpkin, you work so hard.

PUMPKIN

My poor back be stabbat harful bya enna da day.

DAME DOROTHY

Because to bury the dead you must dig deep.

PUMPKIN

Head-high from da bottom a da hole.

DAME DOROTHY

Poor Thomas, in the ground.
After he's gone, we'll dig nothing deeper than the two-foot pit a seed-potato needs. Little rows of vegetables, on our small and fertile farm.

PUMPKIN

Fuck be dat. Bin a gentleman farmer den, own da biggest farm fer miles, hire some poor lob ta plant da vegetals fer me. 'N' da machines ta dig limestone from da quarry.

(Silence. Dorothy looks away.)

DAME DOROTHY

I hate the quarry.

PUMPKIN

You make a swollot a money outa dat quarry.

DAME DOROTHY

Nothing good will come from it.

PUMPKIN

Limestone come from it.

DAME DOROTHY

Those women in the kitchen. Did you see them?

PUMPKIN

Ah, nope.

DAME DOROTHY

Three ranter women.

PUMPKIN

Ranters bin heretics.

DAME DOROTHY

They used to live in cottages on a farm—on the land Thomas's father bought, where Thomas dug the quarry. They had a little farm there.

PUMPKIN

Stupid a dem to do dat, set a farm on dat rocky soil. You shouldn'ta oughta take dem in, dey han't gonna wanna leave. 'N' steal yer eyes out yer sockets. 'N' got contagious lice.

DAME DOROTHY

I have a dream almost every night. Thomas has died and his soul gone off to the judgment seat. And been damned, poor Thomas. He looks for hell, but he can't find the entrance. Then he does find it, and it's at the bottommost pit in the quarry. There's a sinkhole, like a drain, small, and he slips down it and disappears. And sometimes the dream doesn't end there. Sometimes I'm being pulled in after him.

PUMPKIN

'Tis silly.

DAME DOROTHY

Their cottages were burnt when the land was seized. They sleep in ditches.
None of the children will come home to see him die.

(From offstage there is a voice calling:)

DOGWATER

D-d-Dame D-Dorothy! Duh-duh-duh-Dame Duh-Dorothy!

PUMPKIN

Shit beans, it's da pastor!

(They scramble to respectable dress and distance as Dogwater bursts in.)

DR. DOGWATER

Good morning, Dame Dorothy. How's the puh-patient? Improving?

DAME DOROTHY

Quite the opposite.

DR. DOGWATER

Optimism, optimism—he's resting puh-puh-peacefully.

DAME DOROTHY

He's nearly dead.

DR. DOGWATER

Ah. Tuh-too bad. I hope he's resigned.
Have you had a chuh-chance to look over those papers I left?

DAME DOROTHY

I've been preoccupied.

DR. DOGWATER

Yes, this is a tuh-trying time for you, I understand, but buh-business affairs press on, and not even the guh-grim reaper can hold them in abeyance. I suh-speak now, of course, not as your suh-spiritual adviser but as your fuh-future partner in commerce. The quarry expansion depends on your cuh-cooperation.

PUMPKIN

You bin expandet da quarry?

DR. DOGWATER

Huh-who are you?

PUMPKIN

Da new gravedigger, namet Pumpkin.

DR. DOGWATER

Aha. And you're interested in quarrying, Mr. Pumpkin?

PUMPKIN

Ah, yup. I bin verra interested in da development a industry.

DR. DOGWATER

Splendid! And so you shuh-should be! A tuh-true man of the age! You're a Protestant, of course.

PUMPKIN

Yessir, I always bin dat.

DR. DOGWATER

You see before you, Dame Duh-Dorothy, luh-living proof of my contention: that the vuh-violent and irruptive nah-nah-nature of these times is no cause for despair. Leave despair to the weak and the gah-gaseous, to the Catholics. You were born poor?

PUMPKIN

In da verra bogs a deprivation.

DR. DOGWATER

And now you're a puh-puh-prospering gravedigger!

PUMPKIN

I han't exactly prospering but—

DR. DOGWATER

But you'll keep duh-digging till you reach your puh-pot of gold, right?
How rich do you thuh-think Sir Thomas Browne was, Puh-Pumpkin? Very rich?

PUMPKIN

Ah, yup.

DR. DOGWATER

Enormously rich?

DAME DOROTHY

Dr. Dogwater, this is hardly an appropriate time to be counting my husband's money.

DR. DOGWATER

It's instructive, Muh-Mrs. Browne. Pumpkin, this man was—uh, *is* extremely wealthy. You could bury the entire parish and nuh-not earn half of what he makes in one day just luh-lying here and letting his puh-puh-profits accumulate. He's puh-practically muh-made of gold. Do you want to be rich like that, Pumpkin?

PUMPKIN

I haspire to dat, pastor, ef I work fer it—

DR. DOGWATER

Once we thought Heaven glowed with the light of divine fire, Dame Dorothy, but now we *know*—it glows with the shine of gold. In the fuh-firmament, a suh-sun of gold that makes men like this man tuh-twitch, and writhe, and work. You wuh-worry about expanding the quarry and dislocating squatters, but here is my argument made flesh—this man. Scrape the lichen from the rock, expose it to the rays of that muh-muh-metal sun, give it guh-gainful employment, and watch it grow into something more nuh-noble than suh-suh-scum.

PUMPKIN

So you gonna expandet da quarry?

DR. DOGWATER

I am not accustomed to discussing my business with hired help. Good day.

(Pause.)

PUMPKIN

I bin going. Pastor. I appreciatet da instructet. Missus.

(He goes.)

DAME DOROTHY

There was no cause for impoliteness, Dr. Dogwater, you shouldn't have spoken so abruptly.

DR. DOGWATER

You have a suh-soft heart, Dame Dorothy, and that befits a wuh-woman, but after Sir Thomas is d . . . is d . . . d . . . d . . .

DAME DOROTHY

Dead.

DR. DOGWATER

. . . and keeping the cuh-company of angels in puh-paradise you will be chuh-chief shareholder in the Nuh-nuh-Norfolk and London Limestone Quarrying Company. And you will need a sterner, more ruh-rigorous mien. Your huh-husband lacked that. He hoarded gold, too timid in the muh-marketplace.

DAME DOROTHY

He was fearful of loss.

DR. DOGWATER

Wuh-well put. But God hates idle money as much as he hates idle men. Suh-Sir Thomas could not be muh-moved to reinvest in the buh-business. We hope his widow will—

DAME DOROTHY

Could we discuss this another time.

DR. DOGWATER

Of course. Thoughtless of me. After the fuh-funeral. Tomorrow, perhaps.

DAME DOROTHY

And we really don't know if the shares have been left to me, or if they've been left to anyone at all. If there's no Will—

DR. DOGWATER

If there's no wuh-wuh . . . OF COURSE THERE'S A WUH-WILL. Uh isn't there?

DAME DOROTHY

I have no idea. He loves making messes, leaving them behind.

DR. DOGWATER

Muh-much more than a muh-mess! The Buh-Book of the Apocalypse couldn't compare. The cuh-crown will confiscate the entire estate, the cuh-quarry would become cuh-crown lands, the kuh-king, long may he reign, is a vuh-veritable muh-muh-Mammon, ah-ah-avaricious! He's appropriating absolutely everything he can get his guh-greedy ruh-royal mitts on, we'll all be ah-utterly utterly utterly destroyed if Browne dies without a Will! Puh-Panic! Puh-Panic! He'll have to tell us where it is, or write a new one.

DAME DOROTHY

He won't write anything anymore. He says the smell of ink makes him nauseous.

DR. DOGWATER

But Dame Dorothy he's a writer.

DAME DOROTHY

Apparently no longer.

DR. DOGWATER

Duh-Dame Dorothy, this is no joke. We have to get him to tell us where he put the document
(Screaming very loudly) WHEN HE WAKES UP!

(Dr. Browne wakes with a start.)

DAME DOROTHY

Doctor Dogwater!

DR. BROWNE

Am I dead?

DAME DOROTHY

No, Thomas.

HIS SOUL

(Appearing) NO! NO! NO! *(It disappears again)*

DR. BROWNE

There are moles tunneling underneath this house. I can hear them, burrowing. They are undermining the foundation. Fetch the mole dogs. Where's the gravedigger? He was here. Has the urn arrived?

DAME DOROTHY

Not yet.

DOGWATER

Uh-urn?

DR. BROWNE

Excavated. In the digging. Right there in the quarry, a mound of some sort. An urn in the heart of it. Containing hair, teeth and bones. No idea whose remains. Saxon, maybe. Roman, perhaps. Perhaps earlier even than that . . .
(To Dogwater) Who are you? Dorothy, who *is* this man?

DAME DOROTHY

It's Dr. Dogwater, Thomas, you know Dr. Dogw—

DR. BROWNE

A doctor? Can he do something about the moles? Is this your leech?

(Browne plucks Schadenfreude's leech, now swollen, from beneath his nightshirt and tosses it to Dogwater, who catches it, then realizes what he's holding.)

DR. DOGWATER

Luh-luh-luh-LEEEECH!

(Dogwater flings the leech into the audience.)

DAME DOROTHY

Thomas, it's Dr. Dogwater, your pastor, your old, old friend.

DR. DOGWATER

And buh-business puh-puh-partner. L-Leviticus Dogwater.

(Browne glares at Dogwater without recognition.)

DR. BROWNE

I never saw you before.

DAME DOROTHY

Thomas!

DOGWATER

Oh, d-dear, he's l-lost his wuh-wits.

DR. BROWNE

I studied embryology with Fabricius in Padua, Doctor whoever-you-are; the great Fabricius, did you know that? The chick in the egg. The baby in the . . . the genesis of things.
I was a physician but I stuck to research. I couldn't cure people. Christ did that, or so they say. Well, I'm sure he did. I couldn't. I wrote things . . .
My experiments led me from embryology to engineering to excavation to urns and my current fascination with burial . . . customs.
(Little pause)
Unearth the urn,
pop it open
with a pick,
remove the skull:
crack it, brown,
like a nut, and
in the bowl, in the
seat
of the soul . . .
not even dust.
Just the tattered white filaments

of some spidery event.
(Little pause)
It is impossible
to conclude
anything.
I know who you are, Dogwater.

DR. DOGWATER

Hah-how are you today, Sir Thomas?

DR. BROWNE

Mortal.

DR. DOGWATER

Muh-muh-muh—

DR. BROWNE

And fading. I cannot shit. All plugged up; no place to go.

DR. DOGWATER

I will puh-pray for you.

DR. BROWNE

I'd sell my soul for a bowel movement.

HIS SOUL

You would! I know you would! You never valued me!

DR. DOGWATER

Tuh-Thomas, we were just tah-talking and wuh-wondering if your wuh-Will had buh-been completed.

DR. BROWNE

My Will.

DR. DOGWATER

Y-yes. Nuh-now is the time to be letting guh-go of worldly things, tuh-turning your thoughts to suh-salvation and the uh-unimaginable delights of puh-puh-puh-paradise.

(His Soul rattles its chains wistfully.)

DR. BROWNE

Paradise.

HIS SOUL

Paradise! You keep me from paradise, you swollen stinkbag, wormfood—die!

(It goes away.)

DR. BROWNE

You want to know if I've made a Will.

DR. DOGWATER

Yes.

DR. BROWNE

Did I, Dorothy?

DAME DOROTHY

I think so, yes.

DR. BROWNE

(To Dogwater) Yes.

DR. DOGWATER

Guh-good. Nuh-now I—

DR. BROWNE

You want to know where the Will is.

DR. DOGWATER

Wuh-well, I—

DR. BROWNE

I have no idea.

DR. DOGWATER

Tuh-Thomas, this is nah-nah-not a juh-joking mah-mah-mah—

DR. BROWNE

When I was a medical student in Padua, I often visited the Jewish Ghetto there. Because I wanted to know if it was true.

(Small pause.)

DR. DOGWATER

Wha . . . What's true?

DR. BROWNE

If it was true what they say about old Jews dying.
Do you know what they say about old Jews dying?

DR. DOGWATER

Nah-nah—

DR. BROWNE

Dorothy, do you know?

DAME DOROTHY

Where's the Will, Thomas? Dr. Dogwater wants to see it.

DR. BROWNE

They say when an old Jew is about to die, and he wants to be left . . . *alone* . . . with his Deity, he turns his face to the wall.

(Dr. Browne does this. There is silence.)

DR. BROWNE

The other Jews understand this to be a sign that they should absent themselves.

DAME DOROTHY

Thomas—

DR. BROWNE

And they *do*. They *leave*.

(Dame Dorothy and Dr. Dogwater look at each other.)

DAME DOROTHY

Perhaps we should leave.

DR. DOGWATER

But he isn't Jewish.

(Babbo bursts in, carrying an unbaked tart.)

BABBO

Secuse me again, Mrs. Browne, but dem three knacky women in da kitchen bin movet to da pantry now 'n' be coombin over da silver 'n'one stufftet halfta da tea service in her pockets.

DR. DOGWATER

Thieves!

DAME DOROTHY

Not thieves, just three harmless ranter women . . .

DR. DOGWATER

Ruh-ranters!? What are ruh-ranters doing in your house?

BABBO

Well right now dey bin stealet evahthing dat han't bin screwed down 'r locked up.

DAME DOROTHY

They were hungry, it was cold last night, I . . .

DR. DOGWATER

A sterner mien, Mrs. Browne! Ruh-ranters are debauched heretics. Cuh-come. We'll see to this puh-pillaging together. Buh-buh-Browne, your house is in duh-duh-disarray. Remember, God expects Man to d . . . to d . . . to d . . .

DR. BROWNE

To die.

DR. DOGWATER

Just so. In a responsible and ah-orderly fah-fah-fashion.

(Dogwater and Dame Dorothy go. Babbo starts to follow them.)

DR. BROWNE

Halt, imponderably old and faithful retainer.

BABBO

Me?

DR. BROWNE

(Searching under the mattress) Who else? I want you to hide something.

(He produces the Will, a slender document wax-sealed, lawyer-stamped, wrapped in black ribbon and bordered in black.)

BABBO

Bin you writet another book?

DR. BROWNE

God forbid.

BABBO

Hamen ta dat.

DR. BROWNE

My Will. Everyone's clamoring for a copy, it's the most popular thing I ever wrote. Hide it, Babbo, I'll let you know when it's wanted. Hide it well.

(Babbo crams the Will inside the tart.)

DR. BROWNE

Oh. Well . . . um, alright, you . . . You'll, uh . . . remember to take it out before you bake it.

BABBO

A course, Doctah, I bin old but my memory bin sharp as a . . . Sharp as a . . . Uh . . .

DR. BROWNE

Tack?

BABBO

Right! So han't be worret, Doctah Greene.

DR. BROWNE

Browne.

BABBO

Da tarts come out nicet. Gotta go get da chickens ready fer broasting.

(She goes.
His Soul sits up.)

HIS SOUL

Can't you release me? Can't you let me go? You see how I suffer.

DR. BROWNE

(Trying) I can't . . . unclench.

HIS SOUL

You hoard everything. It's only justice that you should die of constipation.

DR. BROWNE

Don't hate me so terribly.

HIS SOUL

I want a divorce.

DR. BROWNE

I fed you well. I read Latin and Greek, philosophy and mathematics, all for you. All food for you.

HIS SOUL

You tried. It never worked. Everything had to pass through you. All that meat. We must divide possessions now, and part company.

DR. BROWNE

I picked wildflowers, I gawped at the moon, I prayed devotedly to God for your redemption—

HIS SOUL

Redeem me then. DIE! I want nothing weighty, no ballast when I ascend. Nothing you've touched and polluted. The house, the gold, the quarry, all yours. I only want a small shard of an idea.

DR. BROWNE

I thought . . . I thought I'd *want* to die today but I'm so . . . afraid. Don't leave me.

HIS SOUL

You used to be able to close your eyes and see the light of Heaven.

DR. BROWNE

That was very long ago.

HIS SOUL

I know. Now when you close your eyes . . .

DR. BROWNE

A kind of dull brown and red darkness.

HIS SOUL

Mostly that, yes, but—

DR. BROWNE

Daylight diffused through flesh. Nothing else.

HIS SOUL

Liar! There's one small speck of fire in there, one pure dot of light flickering, imperiled, but there!

DR. BROWNE

Paradise.

HIS SOUL

You try to hide it from me!

DR. BROWNE

Reduced to that pinprick.

HIS SOUL

But paradise even so! Mine!

DR. BROWNE

I'll have to think about it.

HIS SOUL

Don't think! Don't do that! Just give! If you think you'll extinguish it! Relinquish it to me!

DR. BROWNE

Paradise. *(He's beginning to nod out)* What do I think of Paradise? Listen. The machines. Boooomm. Booooom . . .
Parad . . .

(He's asleep.)

HIS SOUL

Miser! After all I've done for you! You have to examine even that, that one atomie of gold; never valued it before, but now that I want it, you can't resist fingering it till it's tarnished, cheap brass like all the other goods in your cobwebbed musty little brass shop. Brazen hoarder. I hope you burst.

(As His Soul is railing the ranter women have snuck in and gathered round the bed.)

SARAH

(Looking at His Soul) Bin talket to his soul.

(His Soul sinks from view.)

MARY

What it say?

RUTH

Say liberty. Say justice fer all da fellow creatures, Mary. Say peace 'n' food 'n' land, 'n' whilst it weepet fer da homeless 'n' afflictet dis windgall here get bored 'n' fall asleep.

SARAH

Muttering paradise.

RUTH

Be a good time ta rant, 'n' set up a hoo-hah dat shake da thatch from da roof 'n' buggle da peeps from out his yead. 'N' do it now. Da louse be dead before you knowit. 'N' dat pastor almost took us pinching da silver.

SARAH

I got a lovely big spoon. Verra pretty spoon.

RUTH

(Beginning to rant) By da verra balls a da bleedet Christ, by da withered dugs a Mary, by da stripet socks a Joseph . . .

(All three start to shake in the grip of something powerful. Mary snaps out of it and stops Ruth.)

MARY

Hold it, Ruth, fer Christ sake, caused oncet you get ranting all three of us commencet. 'N' Sarah ent said ready. 'N' 'tis fer da memory a her poor mama we come here.

(Browne stirs.)

SARAH

Da puffball squirmet, be waket soon. Him dreamet some foul, sweaty dream, some guilty racket him.
Soon we rant, not yet. I gotta feel da time.

RUTH

(Hissing in Browne's ear) Earfen clot.

MARY

Hist Ruth, 'n' come away.

(They exit.)

DR. BROWNE

(Waking slowly) There's a ship on a dark river, fed by frozen streams, feeding an arctic ocean; my coffin ship. It's creaking. *(He calls to His Soul)* Are you there? Can we . . . negotiate? Leave me then. Losing you is less than losing nothing, you incorporeal nonentity.
Maccabbee! MACCABBEE!
I mustn't shout, it—

(Maccabbee enters.)

MACCABBEE

Whatchoo want?

DR. BROWNE

A final experiment. Fetch three live chickens and—

MACCABBEE

You oughta rest, converse yer strength, Dr. Browne, keep da experiments fer later—

DR. BROWNE

My later is gone. I have to know . . . something. Fetch three live chickens.

MACCABBEE

Three live chickens.

DR. BROWNE

Weigh each one.

MACCABBEE

Weigh each one.

DR. BROWNE

Then strangle them.

MACCABBEE

A course.

DR. BROWNE

Wait a few minutes after they die, and then weigh them again. Bring me the results.

MACCABBEE

Da strangled chickens?

DR. BROWNE

No, *cretin*. The weights. Pre- and postmortem weights.

MACCABBEE

No need ta call names.

DR. BROWNE

Chicken A weighs . . . six pounds. Alive.
Does it weigh less when it's dead?
If it does, then something . . . has been lost.
If it weighs the same dead as alive then it has lost . . . nothing at all. Nothing of substance.

MACCABBEE

What could it lose?

DR. BROWNE

It could lose . . . its soul.

MACCABBEE

Awww, Dr. Browne, dat's nuts. Chickens han't got souls.

DR. BROWNE

It has some vital spirit, some ether that impells its heart to beat, some shock or force; call it what you will, but there's nothing living without that . . . And I must know its weight, the awful weight of the soul, before . . .

MACCABBEE

Before what, Dr. Browne?

DR. BROWNE

Nothing. You're right. It is . . . nuts. I . . .
Why is there no one here to comfort me?
I'm swelling. Leave me. But . . . Maccabbee.

MACCABBEE

What, Dr. Browne?

DR. BROWNE

Keep your eyes on the ground. Watch for little holes.

MACCABBEE

???

DR. BROWNE

Mole holes. Tunnel mouths. A mixture of cyanide and boiling lye . . .
Get out of here.
The chicken experiment. Do it. I'm . . . already underway, and I have to know . . .
The ropes on the dock are slipping from the moorings, and I'm . . . off . . .

(He's off, unconscious.)

MACCABBEE

Fetch da rottet birds, pickle dis gamey fish, count da ribs a dat poison snake, strangle three chickens. Maybe when he's dead I'll go help da German cut up his cadavers. Science bin slavery. 'N' ent one a dem knows how ta cure my clap.

(Dr. Browne begins to rattle.)

MACCABBEE

Doctah?

(Rattle.)

MACCABBEE

Doctah?

(A really alarming gasp, then a huge expulsion of breath, and the lights begin to change slowly and the death music is heard.)

MACCABBEE

Dat soundet like da terminal hexpiration ta me. Before noon, like I prognosticated. Funny dere were no last words, he was always so talkative.

(Death enters, growling, with his carving knife at the ready. His Soul sits up as the ladder to heaven appears.
Maccabbee senses something creepy afoot and slinks out, frightened. Death approaches the bed and His Soul reaches up toward the ladder. A hooded figure—The Abbess of X—enters stealthily.)

HIS SOUL

I begin to climb; I have far to go; with every rung the weight of your contamination will fall from me, like a moulting bird I lessen and lighten and loose these chains . . .

DEATH

Thomas . . . my child, the bitter hour, the wasting hour has come. I come for you, I ache for you, lamentable, lamentable, I . . . your flesh, sweet heart, to rend at last . . .

THE ABBESS OF X

(She is aware of neither Death nor His Soul) Thomas?

HIS SOUL

To Paradise!

THE ABBESS OF X

THOMAS!

DEATH

Mine, flower, mine . . .

THE ABBESS OF X

God in Heaven, I've come too late.

(She takes out a breviary, a rosary, a vial of holy water, and begins to murmur the Extreme Unction, in Latin.)

DR. BROWNE

Father . . .

DEATH

(Raising his knife) Thomas . . .

DR. BROWNE

Father . . .

HIS SOUL

Good-bye!

DR. BROWNE

Fa . . . ther . . . in to your hands . . .

HIS SOUL

Say it!

DR. BROWNE

Into your hands I . . .

THE ABBESS OF X

Thomas. Thomas, can you hear me? Where's the Will, Thomas? Who did you name in The Will!?

HIS SOUL

(Prompting) COMMEND . . . MY . . .

DR. BROWNE

MY . . . I COMMEND MY . . .
(Hearing what His Soul is prompting him toward) NO! I . . . *CONDEMN* MY . . . SPIR—

HIS SOUL

NO!

DR. BROWNE

(Forcing himself awake) NO!

(Dr. Browne sits up violently. He sees the Abbess—HE SCREAMS! He turns to see Death with his raised knife—HE REALLY SCREAMS! Death screams and with a growl runs away. The music scratches off with the sound of a needle swept off a phonograph record. The lights bump back and the Abbess rolls under the bed seconds before Dame Dorothy, Dr. Dogwater and Babbo run in. His Soul is stunned at the sudden reversal.)

HIS SOUL

HOW!? HOW!? YOU WERE DEAD, YOU HAD DIED, YOU'D TURNED TO CLAY, WHAT RESUSCITATED YOU?

(His Soul slips behind the bed. The ladder disappears.)

DAME DOROTHY

Thomas, can you hear me? Are you alright?

DR. BROWNE

I . . . am . . . not . . . sure . . .

BABBO

Praise be, praise be, bin snatchet from da grinning yawp a doom!

DR. BROWNE

My sister was here.

DAME DOROTHY

No, Thomas, your sister is dead.

DR. BROWNE

But she was here. She spoke Latin and sprinkled water, and look, the pillow is wet.

DR. DOGWATER

Tuh-Thomas, y-your suh-sister d-d . . . perished in a shuh-shuh-shuh-shuh-shipwreck. Y-years ago. Duh-drowned.

DR. BROWNE

But she was here. Resurrected. With . . . him.

DAME DOROTHY

There's no one here, Thomas.

DR. BROWNE

And he's been dead longer than she. He had the knife, I remember that knife. Old monster.

DAME DOROTHY

Dr. Dogwater, what's he talking about?

DR. DOGWATER

Bah-bah-bah . . . I duh-duh-don't . . .

DR. BROWNE

(After a little pause, listening, then) Another ship . . . from warmer seas . . . is sailing here . . . for me.
And listen, the machines. Hard at work. Moving earth. Boooom. Boooom. Boooom. Boooom.
To beat
the little
gentle man
who comes
to undo.
(He's out)

DR. DOGWATER

I-is he . . . ?

(Dr. Dogwater tiptoes up to Browne, and gently pinches Browne's nostrils shut; Browne starts snoring through his mouth.)

DAME DOROTHY

The engines give me nightmares and headaches. But they tranquilize him.

DR. DOGWATER

Wuh-once, he b-bade me listen to the sound. The puh-pounding sound they make. Buh-boom. Buh-booom. Luh-listen, Dogwater, he s-said. Guh-God's timpani. Buh-booom.
I thought I'd use that ah-anecdote in the eu-eu-eulogy. Buh-booom.
Cuh-call me if he wuh-wakes. Wh-when he does. We've guh-got to find out about that wuh-wuh-wuh-Will.

(Dogwater leaves. Babbo and Dame Dorothy sit, watching Dr. Browne sleep.
The three ranter women enter, sit quietly around the bed. They look at Dame Dorothy and she looks at them, and everyone looks at the dying man.
His Soul sits up and begins to sing softly.)

HIS SOUL

(Singing:)
There is a little house in Heaven
Built of brick and wood,
In a shady and restricted
Crime-free neighborhood.
The shutters and the doors are painted
Bright cerulean blue;
And vines of morning glories climb,
Bloom-eternal in their prime,
Free of gravity and time,
Purple-white and fresh with dew,
Flower-mouth of Very-God
The Day does not divide in two.

And here in Heaven
I will never die.
I can say that
And not feel
I'm telling
A lie.
In Heaven I will never die.
Never
Never
Never
Die.

Act Two

IN WHAT TORNE SHIP SOEVER I EMBARKE

The Hard Light of Later Morning, the Glare of Noon

Dame Dorothy, the three ranter women, and Babbo watch Dr. Browne, who is asleep.

MARY

(With glowing gentleness) Da kingdom a God be da kingdom a da earf. Dere bin no Heaven and no Hell, but only dis: da doings a da fellow creatures as dey dwell in dis world. Dat's what da ranters say. When Christ come again he come inta da flesh a wimmin 'n' da flesh a men, 'n' den all dat walk be good 'n' golden creatures 'n' kind. Dat's what da ranters say.

RUTH

Quarry land bin common land fer alla way back to da Garden a Heden, 'n' I care not a pin ner a fart fer his paper a ownership. What own? My little cottage burnet. My shitten rocky farm dug up. Now dey say, ef you wanna eat go work fer da swollen stench Browne and his devil digs. Fuck be dat.

SARAH

My ma bin a witch, Dame Dorothy, a forest witch. Han't been much good at it; mostly deliver babbies with a coupla harmless tricks. Dat's all. A good fellow creature 'n' ranter; she teachet me, 'n' we livet inna woods by Bury St. Edmunds till dey encloset da woods, 'n' den da trouble come.

DAME DOROTHY

Bury St. Edmunds.

SARAH

You know dat name.
My ma curset da squire dat bought da woods, 'n' even though she han't got no talent 'n' her curses nevah carry, da squire go white 'n' freaket, 'n' his yeart stop beatet, 'n' he die, 'n' dey arrest my ma 'n' dis other woman fer witchcraft. 'N' dat other woman bin lessa a witch den my ma, she han't even call herself a witch, bin just a woman.

DAME DOROTHY

Your mother was—

SARAH

(Nodding) 'N' no one think more'n a flogging's likely, since dey han't hung a witch fer forty year, but den dey call fer a witness inna trial; a great thinker 'n' man a words, a doctor.

DAME DOROTHY

Oh God.

SARAH

Just bin knightet by da king. Bin a sir.

(Silence. They all look at Browne.)

SARAH

'N' he talket, talket like a angel sing, but his words bin wicked, twisty words, 'n' bya time he shut his yatch dey got my ma swinget by a rough old rope. 'N' dat bin da enna my mama on dis earf.

DAME DOROTHY

Please. He was used. He never intended that. He thought he was raising a few harmless points, minor theological speculation. He came home with a fever, he didn't sleep for weeks.

SARAH

Dat happent ten year ago. 'N' last week we bin headet fer da wilds a Scotland; my ma come ta me 'n' say: "Sarah, turn about 'n' vistet him on his deathbed. Bring him a blessting from me."

DAME DOROTHY

But your mother—

SARAH

(Fierce) Bin dead.
(A smile) She bin a poor witch. I be much more talentet.

MARY

Sarah hear things.

RUTH

Talket to her mama nightly. 'Tis verra peculiar.

DAME DOROTHY

We should leave this room.

RUTH

Time to rant yet, Sarah?

SARAH

Soon, soon.

DAME DOROTHY

Rant? What do you mean, rant?

(Little pause.)

RUTH

Back to da kitchen. Da smella him maket me queasious, he gotta cheesy color inna face 'n' stinket sumpin wharfle.

MARY

(Softly, looking at Browne) Weep fer da travails a da flesh, fellow creatures. We bin all headet fer dat mordal day bed 'n' dat earfen hole.

RUTH

Soon . . .

(Mary and Ruth exit.)

DAME DOROTHY

He never meant to harm. You could carve that on his gravestone. He was never kind.
(To Thomas) I've seen you feel . . . remorse. That's something. But . . . You did not live well upon this earth, Thomas.

(Dorothy exits. Sarah lags behind.)

BABBO

Verra. 'Tis not his fault he bin a stingy 'n' raptious blabbermouth, 'r' dat yer knacky ma got hanget.

SARAH

You watchet him good.

BABBO

You keepet yer hands offa my tarts 'n' chickens.

SARAH

All food belonget to all fellow creatures.

BABBO

Dat food fer aftah da funeral.

SARAH

Aftah da funeral, dey han't gonna feel much like eating.

BABBO

You don't know dese people. Dey will.

SARAH

Wait 'n' see. Dey han't gonna wanna eat.

(She goes.)

BABBO

Dose wimmin gonna snitch da nails outa da floorboards. Such a perturbet. Inna holden days, death bin a little do in da village a hanimals. Da moriens bin movet by da hoven fer warmth, 'r by a winda if dey had a fever 'n' wantet da coolth a da breezet. 'N' a soft moaning 'n' da tears flow, 'n' da world go on. Not hacta so perturbet, like da world bin ending, like today.

(The Abbess crawls out from under the bed, across from where Babbo is sitting. Babbo sees her stand.)

BABBO

A hesprit!

(They regard each other.)

BABBO

Ah, hesprit, my old scaley eyes bin disconceiving me; you bin a phantasm in da pocket a my grief, 'r else you be da ghost a poor drownet Alice Browne. Can you speak?

THE ABBESS OF X

Babbo.

BABBO

You speaket . . . my name! Den you be da verra ghost a poor dear Alice. But tell me, hesprit, how come you bin dresset like a nun?

THE ABBESS OF X

Old woman. I was, I . . . am Alice Browne, but no ghost.

BABBO

Ah, nope? Bin you a vampire, 'r sumpin like dat, den?

THE ABBESS OF X

I'm not dead.

BABBO

Den you bin alive.

THE ABBESS OF X

Yes.

BABBO

Den you han't drownet on dat ship?

THE ABBESS OF X

No.

BABBO

But . . . We all thought you'd drownet.

THE ABBESS OF X

You were wrong.

(Pause.)

BABBO

You gotta hexplanation?

THE ABBESS OF X

The ship sank. The sea was merciless. We had barely cleared Yarmouth harbor. Everyone on board perished, except myself.

BABBO

How bin you savet, Alice?

THE ABBESS OF X

I swam.

BABBO

Back ta Yarmouth?

THE ABBESS OF X

To France.

BABBO

You swam alla way to France!?

THE ABBESS OF X

Yes.

BABBO

But Alice, you han't know howta swim.

THE ABBESS OF X

I know. I was spared by the benevolent hand of God.

BABBO

(Awestruck) Verra?

THE ABBESS OF X

There were typhoons, Babbo, and great forked bolts of lightning, and fish with teeth! I thought my end had come. But I was rescued . . . by a vision.

BABBO

Sweet tootha da Virgin! A vision?

THE ABBESS OF X

An angel of God preceded me through the brine, dog-paddling. With an iron sword wrapped all in thorns and flaming hair.

BABBO

Red hair?

THE ABBESS OF X

Flaming hair, Babbo.
I learned to dog-paddle by emulating him, and when I grew too weary I clung to the hem of his heavenly raiment and he towed me to the beach at Boulogne.

BABBO

Well. Dat be sumpin, Alice.

THE ABBESS OF X

And on the beach the angel said, "Alice Browne, as you have clung to me, cling to the Holy and Apostolic Catholic Church, cleave to it, and in its clefts you will be safe from perils worse than drowning." I was summoned to turn my back on the great and perfidious Apostasy of my native land and seek, on foreign shores, the sweet succor of the One True Faith.

BABBO

But why han't you told us dat, Alice? Da doctah grievet long 'n' fulbous fer da lossa his sistah, 'n' we all did, 'n' whilst us weepet 'n' wet you bin a safet 'n' dry French nun. How come you han't write a letter, 'r sumpin'?

THE ABBESS OF X

Our order observes very strict rules of silence.

BABBO

Fer twenty years? What order be dat?

THE ABBESS OF X

I'm . . . not at liberty to say.

(Browne stirs.)

BABBO

He bin waket! Dr. Browne! Look who swimmet da Channel just ta say good-bye.

THE ABBESS OF X

Babbo, hush! If . . . he saw me, the shock could kill him.

BABBO

He bin almost dead anyway.

THE ABBESS OF X

They mustn't know I've returned.

BABBO

Dey han't hold yer being a Catholic against you, Alice. Mrs. Browne bin partial ta heretics; she yacket with three ranters inna kitchen at dis verra minute.

THE ABBESS OF X

I want to give my brother the Extreme Unction, Babbo. I want to try to wrench his wayward soul from the fires of Hell, from everlasting torment and utter damnation.

BABBO

Well a course ya do, but how you gonna do dat?

THE ABBESS OF X

I have a special dispensation from the Archbishop of Anjou to perform last rites for Thomas. I must be at his side when the end comes; it's all a matter of timing.

BABBO

Have a seat, Alice, da wait won't be long.

(Browne stirs again.)

THE ABBESS OF X

The others will come and foul the plan. I need a disguise.

BABBO

Fer carnival last Shrove Tuesday Mrs. Browne 'n' me sewet dis piggie suit fer da doctah ta wear. It bin a hoot. You wanna dresset like a pig, Alice? Dey nevah recognize ya. Dey thought Dr. Browne bin a verra pig.

THE ABBESS OF X

But what would a pig be doing in Thomas's sickroom?

BABBO

Dere bin stranger 'n' dat in here already today 'n' it han't even noon yet.

THE ABBESS OF X

Too conspicuous.

BABBO

I gotta idea.

THE ABBESS OF X

Tell me.

BABBO

Inna village a my youf, whena body bin dying, dere was a old woman sit bya bed, 'n' she knittet da shroud outta soft wool with long bone needles. She bin a harbinger a death, 'n' her clacket sound bin heard all ovah da town. Clackety-clack.

DR. BROWNE

(From far off) It is surprisingly deep here, and below the surface terribly cold, and the pull is treacherous. I am treading . . .

BABBO

Bin waket. Come with me, Alice. Don't die, Doctah, till we get back.

THE ABBESS OF X

Hurry.

(They go.)

DR. BROWNE

(Still far away) Warm me, take me off to warmer lands on your dark timber ship.

(A strange figure, dressed in rags, enters, crosses to the bed. She wears a half-mask of an old, old woman and a black veil. All her clothes are black. It is Doña Estrelita, disguised.)

THE WASHER/DOÑA ESTRELITA

Thomas. Thomas, can you hear me?

DR. BROWNE

(Still far off) Bake me in the sun, dry me in the arrid heat of your . . . *(He's out)*

THE WASHER/DOÑA ESTRELITA

Already I bring warmth.

(She peels back the bedclothes and embraces him.)

THE WASHER/DOÑA ESTRELITA

Can you feel the heat of my heart, Thomas, of my blood?

DR. BROWNE

Thank you, blest redeemer.

THE WASHER/DOÑA ESTRELITA

Be patient. You are split in two. You say yes, you say no. I come to purify.

(She slips away.)

DR. BROWNE

The sun . . . *(He shudders)* . . . clouds over . . .

(The lights change, the music begins, a lesser version of the false alarms in Act One.
Death enters; Browne shudders violently. His Soul sits up, the ladder doesn't appear.)

HIS SOUL

The ladder . . . *(It sees Death)*
Good, let's get this over with.

DEATH

Thomas, we need to touch. You're very warm, fever . . . you burn for me.

HIS SOUL

He burns for you, I burn to leave—do it do it what are you waiting for?

DEATH

I'm very sad. To kill this moment, it will never come again, and yet I ache to kill. I am so . . . *(He sniffs)* so hungry . . . *(Sniffs again)* What's that smell?

HIS SOUL

Eat him! Crack his bones and suck the marrow!

DEATH

Delicious smell . . .
(He moves toward the door)
Hot, moulten fruit. Crust puffing, browning. I wonder . . . what's cooking . . . in the kitchen.
A minute.

(He goes.)

HIS SOUL

No! Here! Come back! You fly, you flit, *you are too easily distracted!* It's amazingly difficult to end a life.

DR. BROWNE

(Opening his eyes) Is he gone?

HIS SOUL

Fraud.

DR. BROWNE

I used to do that as a child. The night men. Close your eyes, pull up the covers, count to ten and they go away. I cannot see that face again.

(Sits up, looks about) Was there a woman here? A dark Spanish woman? Did you see a . . .

HIS SOUL

I'm not your watchdog!

DR. BROWNE

You're not my soul, either, just some malcontented noisy thing, a mere side-effect. Of the blockage.
(He strains to shit. Nothing. He's exhausted)
It's all mine. What's in me is mine. My desire—

HIS SOUL

For everything but Paradise is yours.

DR. BROWNE

My intellect—

HIS SOUL

The cesspool through which every pure and crystal thought is dragged, surfacing smeared with offal. Yours.

DR. BROWNE

My writing.
(Pause)
Mine.

HIS SOUL

Ours.
I sang and your little sausage fingers twitched. Each note transcribed, from the grand high harmonics of Heaven, through me to you, through the clumsy and corruptible mechanisms of your hand to a wiggling pen dipped in black smut. Writing. Transcribed, transmogrified, everything you ingest winds up black smut, compost-producer.

DR. BROWNE

If you really are my soul, it's inappropriate for you to despise me so luxuriously. I am your vessel.

HIS SOUL

My prison. And my one prison-pleasure: loathing you.

DR. BROWNE

Why?

HIS SOUL

For writing. For murdering the song.

DR. BROWNE

I recorded it for posterity!

HIS SOUL

"Posterity." I hate that word almost as much as I hate you. Immortality is what you'd like to say but can't, because you know—

DR. BROWNE

Know what?

HIS SOUL

You betrayed me, you with your filthy little wishes and soiled little dreams and your innumerable, incomprehensible fears! I sang as angels do, golden lifting tones on an unending breath, floating music without inception or decline, music that makes a lie of time, a lie of death, of grief or loss or pain, music free of wall or membrane, top or bottom, direction, shape or meaning. I sang of Immortality and you—

DR. BROWNE

Wrote something else.

HIS SOUL

Yes.

(Little pause.)

DR. BROWNE

My words betrayed me. I wrote . . . what I did not mean to write. I saw the door of Heaven swing wide open, a miracle to see, but when I described what I saw inside, the room had changed, it . . . was rather empty, and . . .

(His Soul has gone.)

DR. BROWNE

Do you hear me? Hello!?
Pity me! You should! The world made me, the word betrayed me, I never wanted to see . . .
You'll be sorry . . . when I'm gone. You will.

(Maccabbee enters, hears Browne talking to himself.)

MACCABBEE

Dr. Browne?

DR. BROWNE

Leave me alone. What do you want from me?

MACCABBEE

I stranglet dem chickens.

DR. BROWNE

(Horrified) You . . . *What?*

MACCABBEE

Like you instructet. I stranglet dem poor chickens.

DR. BROWNE

Well, what do you want me to do? Weep for them? Mourn for them? Why don't you just strangle me too, and let's end this farce, and Babbo can stuff me with persimmons and hazelnuts and roast me in the oven.

MACCABBEE

Dr. Browne, you wannet me ta kill dem birds, 'n' now—

DR. BROWNE

What were the results?

MACCABBEE

Well, before dey was pecking inna dirt 'n' sayet chicken words, 'n' aftah dey just lay still.

DR. BROWNE

Clod! Ape! Answer my question! Did you weigh them?

MACCABBEE

Chicken A weighet three 'n' halfet pound before strangletation, 'n' aftah, three 'n' halfet pound.
Chicken B weighet five pounds before, 'n' aftah weighet five pounds.

DR. BROWNE

(Calling out to his absent Soul) Do you hear that! Identical!

MACCABBEE

I know dat, I'm da one did da strangling.
Chicken C weighet four pounds before I strangle it, 'n' aftah . . .
Weighet eight pounds.

DR. BROWNE

Eight pounds?

MACCABBEE

Ah, yup.

DR. BROWNE

It got . . . heavier?

MACCABBEE

Verra wirret, huh?

DR. BROWNE

You're in error. Weigh it again.

MACCABBEE

Han't mistaket. I bin careful. Bin heavier.

DR. BROWNE

IT CANNOT CONCEIVABLY WEIGH *MORE* DEAD THAN . . .

(Babbo enters with the Abbess, disguised as the Weaver of the Shrouds. She wears a half-mask that transforms her into a frightening looking old woman, dressed in gray rags. She is virtually identical to the The Washer, as if they had bought their masks at the same shop.)

BABBO

Secuse me, Doctah. Dis old lady wannet ta see if you bin inna market for a winding sheet—

DR. BROWNE

Get her out of here!
(He is stricken with a terrible terrible pain in his gut)
Oh mercy. What was that? Something . . . ripped.

THE WEAVER/THE ABBESS OF X

I bin a weaver a shrouds, Doctah Browne, I come from verra far away ta help out wif da unraveling.

DR. BROWNE

I don't need help, I . . .
Oh God, help. I think . . . I'm not doing well at all . . . oh.

MACCABBEE

Ya want me ta get a doctah, Doctah?

DR. BROWNE

(Pain!) OH! OH!

MACCABBEE

I translate dat means yes.

THE WEAVER/THE ABBESS OF X

I'll just set up my knitting 'n' commencet da shroud. I only need da measurements.

(She approaches Browne with a measuring string. He recoils, completely terrified of her, and in horrible pain.)

DR. BROWNE

No shroud! Leave!

THE WEAVER/THE ABBESS OF X

But Doctah, I bin reassuret; I knit, 'n' dah clicka my needles—

BABBO

'N' da sayet a da psalms—

THE WEAVER/THE ABBESS OF X

'N' da psalms, sure, bin verra reassuret. Now . . . *(Again with the string)* You know da twenny-third psalm, fer instance?

DR. BROWNE

(Physical agony, terror!) NO CLICKS! NO PSALMS! Not for me you hyena, go prey on someone else's—

(Death enters, eating a chicken leg.)

DR. BROWNE

(Physical agony, much much more terror!!) Oh, dear God. *You.* *(To the Weaver)* What was that psalm you mentioned?

THE WEAVER/THE ABBESS OF X

Da twenny-third.

DR. BROWNE

Let's hear it.

(Browne lies back, still in horrible pain.)

THE WEAVER/THE ABBESS OF X

Da Lord bin my shepert; I han't go wantet.
He make me restet inna green pastrahs,
He leadet me ta still watahs,
'N' restoret my soul.

(His Soul sits up. Death finishes the meat, chews the bone, licks his fingers.)

THE WEAVER/THE ABBESS OF X

'N' even ef I bin walket through da valley a da shadda a death,
I fearet no hevil.

(Death goes. His Soul sinks. Maccabbee enters with Dogwater.)

MACCABBEE

Here da doctah.

DR. DOGWATER

Buh-Browne? I . . . Are you . . . oh my, you are. Guh-good people, the time has come, let us puh-puh-puh-pray.

(He kneels, everyone kneels with him.)

DR. BROWNE

(Very faint, very weak) Maccabbee.

(Maccabbee goes to him.)

DR. BROWNE

This isn't the doctor I had in mind.

DR. DOGWATER

Our f-father, who art in Heaven, look down, show mercy, on this, your wretched but faithful servant in his final hour, and show him the face of your eternal love—

BABBO

(Simultaneously) Dear Gawd, Dr. Browne bin coming inta yer bosmet, 'n' dose of us who lovet him on earf ask you to hopen a place fer him in da hops a Heaven. He bin mostly a ceerible soul, got his faults like evahbody, 'n' you musset be used to faults, you made so many of dem—

MACCABBEE

(Simultaneously, a bit louder than the others) Our fathah who art in Heaven, fergive dose who trespasset against us. Uhh . . . I do not like thee, Dr. Fell, I know not why, I cannot tell, but dis I know, 'n' know full well, I do not like thee, Dr. Fell. I do not like thee, Dr. Fell, oh bag a guts go burn in Hell, I—

(Sotto voce, under the above hubbub, the Abbess tries to sneak in the Extreme Unction, in Latin.)

DR. DOGWATER

Wh-what was that?

(Silence.)

DR. DOGWATER

Duh-did I hear Luh-Latin?

(Silence. Still on his knees, Dogwater walks toward the Abbess.)

DR. DOGWATER

Cuh-come on, I duh-did. Who was praying in Luh-Latin? You. Old wuh-woman.

THE WEAVER/THE ABBESS OF X

Ah, yoop?

DR. DOGWATER

Who are you?

BABBO

She bin da shroud weaver, Dr. Dogwater.

DR. DOGWATER

She looks fah-fah-familiar. In a fuh-funny way. Cuh-come here.

(The Abbess, on her knees, starts walking away from Dogwater, who, on his knees, pursues.
Dame Dorothy rushes in, sees them kneeling.)

DAME DOROTHY

Oh my God, he's dead.

DR. DOGWATER

Huh-he is?

(Everyone rushes to the bed to check.)

DR. BROWNE

Not yet, but keep praying, I'm working on it.

(Schadenfreude enters.)

DR. SCHADENFREUDE

Move aside, move aside, you'll suffocate him.
(To Dogwater) Please, sir, you're crowding my patient.

DR. DOGWATER

He's *my* pah-pah-parishioner.
Tuh-Thomas, I must speak, and in my vuh-voice you should hear not only muh-me, but the cuh-cuh-community of shareholders I represent, and your wuh-wife and your chuh-children—

DR. BROWNE

Children! Dorothy did the children come?
(To Dogwater) Late as usual, late for everything, heel-draggers, lag-behinds—if they dawdle too much they'll miss my demise.

DAME DOROTHY

You wrote them such furious letters, summoning them. I'm sure they'll come.

(Dogwater tries to interject.)

DR. BROWNE

Half my children died in infancy. Those are the ones I loved. The others grew difficult. Their mother and I made thirteen of them.

DAME DOROTHY

Fourteen.

DR. DOGWATER

Your children, whom you love tenderly, and—

DR. BROWNE

Did they ever appreciate me? Ever show me gratitude? Ever produce grandchildren? HAH!

The line comes to a dead halt. My eldest son. Michael. An honored member of the Royal Academy of Science. *My* experiments they never accepted; I'm told they await *his* reports eagerly. *I'm so proud.* He used to send copies to me, but then he . . . stopped.

DAME DOROTHY

(Controlled fury) You told him they were dull.

DR. BROWNE

(The same back at her) They were.

DAME DOROTHY

(The same back at him) Well then, he stopped sending them. You got what you wanted.

DR. DOGWATER

(Exploding) MUH-MAY I PUH-PLEASE FUH-FUH-FUH-FINISH!

(Silence.)

DR. DOGWATER

The Wuh-Will, Sir Thomas, I muh-must know where you puh-put it.

DR. SCHADENFREUDE

I'd like to have a look at it myself, actually.

DR. DOGWATER

Y-you? May I ask whuh-why?

DR. SCHADENFREUDE

Peruse the funeral arrangements. I want time to prepare.

DR. DOGWATER

Prepare whuh-what?

DR. SCHADENFREUDE

The eulogy.

DR. DOGWATER

The eul-lah-lah . . .

DR. SCHADENFREUDE

Eu-lo-gy.

DR. BROWNE

Dorothy, please tell them all to go away.

DR. DOGWATER

Wuh-wait. Am I to uh-understand that yuh-you are to be the eulogist at the fah-funeral? Y-*you*?

DR. SCHADENFREUDE

I would imagine myself the likeliest candidate.

DR. DOGWATER

Suh-Sir Thomas, is this indeed the cuh-case?

DR. BROWNE

You can both eulogize me. Simultaneously. I won't have to listen.

DAME DOROTHY

It's time for everyone to leave. Now.

DR. DOGWATER

Nuh-no. You disappoint me, Suh-Sir Thomas. Not only have you abrogated your fuh-financial committments, but now you intend to abdicate your suh-spiritual commitments as well and allow yourself to be eu-eu-eulogized by a duh-damned hack Heh-Hessian physician?

DR. SCHADENFREUDE

Hack? You call me a *hack*?

DR. DOGWATER

Wuh-well, Browne isn't suh-sterling evidence of your muh-medical competence, is he? Duh-doctors who know what they're duh-doing are usually suh-spared eulogizing their puh-patients.

DR. SCHADENFREUDE

He wasn't killed by my treatments.

DR. DOGWATER

He wasn't cuh-cured by them either.

DR. SCHADENFREUDE

He probably grew that tumor sitting through too many fuh-fuh-four hour suh-suh-sermons, puh-puh-puh-Preacher.

(Deadly silence.)

DR. DOGWATER

(Hurt, with dignity) Duh-do you mock me? My ah-affliction? It doesn't injure me, n-not a buh-bit. I nuh-know that stupid, simple men like yourself suh-snigger behind my back. You say, "What good's a puh-preacher with a stuh-stutter?" You suh-sneer. But I remind you: Muh-muh-Moses stuttered. It is from God my stuh-stutter comes. With every huh-hitch and slip I fuh-feel his hot and angry love. Guh-God loves me. He loves my stuh-stutter. But what does he fuh-feel about *you,* Heh-Herr Doktor? Th-Thomas, this is what comes of your irresponsibility. I huh-hope you're puh-pleased.

(He leaves.)

DAME DOROTHY

Oh dear.

DR. BROWNE

I seem to have lost center stage. May I make a small request?

DAME DOROTHY

What, Thomas?

DR. BROWNE

I want a bath.
I am . . . astonishingly malodorous. A blossom of putrescence.

DR. SCHADENFREUDE

I'd noticed. As though you'd begun to rot ahead of schedule.

DAME DOROTHY

No, Thomas, a bath would give you a chill.

DR. BROWNE

I wouldn't mind a good shiver, one that comes from the temperature of water, rather than from . . . other things. I miss the little creature comforts: spring air, being thin, food, excrement. I would like a bath.

BABBO

You want I should get da sponge, Mrs. Browne, 'n' da bastin?

DAME DOROTHY

You have other work to do.

BABBO

Ah, nope, da chickens been broastin and da tarts bin . . . *(She screeches)* Doctah! Da tart!

DAME DOROTHY

Babbo please stop babbling about chickens and tarts, have some sense of occasion.

BABBO

But I put da . . . da tart in da hoven and in da tart dere was a . . . was a . . . *(She smacks herself in the head jar her memory)*

DR. BROWNE

Dorothy she's having a fit of some sort—

BABBO

Da Will! *I HID DA WILL IN DA*—

DR. BROWNE

Sssshhh!

DAME DOROTHY

The Will? She hid the Will?

DR. BROWNE

No, no, she means she "did my will"; the addled creature, her charming peasant patois, she's incomprehensible. Go forth, Babbo, and roast. Spice, mince, jolly, jolly.

(Babbo rushes out.)

DR. BROWNE

Maccabbee!

MACCABBEE

You want me ta weigh Chicken C again?

DR. BROWNE

Precisely.

MACCABBEE

I already hanticipate da houtcome. 'Tis verra wirret stoof.

(Babbo and Maccabbbe leave.)

DR. BROWNE

I am going to bathe. In the river.

DR. SCHADENFREUDE

I forbid it, Sir Thomas, there is still ice in the water, it's barely spring.

DR. BROWNE

(Trying to stand) Help me up, Dorothy.

DAME DOROTHY

You *want* to die.

(Browne stares at her.)

DR. BROWNE

Of course not.
Maybe not.
Maybe . . . I do.
Old woman, you help me.

THE WEAVER/THE ABBESS OF X

Ah no, Sir Thomas, da Lord ferbids us ta hasten da moment a our death. Ya haveta wait fer His hand. I han't help ya.

(The Washer/Doña Estrelita enters.)

DR. BROWNE

It's my last request. *Must I beg for everything?*

THE WASHER/DOÑA ESTRELITA

No.

(All turn to her.)

THE WASHER/DOÑA ESTRELITA

Secuse da interruptet. I come ta help.
I preparet da moriens *(Mŏr·ĭens)*, I bin a washer a dǎ dying and da dead. I purify. I bin sent fer.

DAME DOROTHY

Sent for by whom?

THE WASHER/DOÑA ESTRELITA

By him.

(They look to Thomas, who is staring hard at the Washer.)

DAME DOROTHY

You're mistaken you have the wrong address.

THE WASHER/DOÑA ESTRELITA

Sir Thomas Browne.

DAME DOROTHY

He didn't send for a washer of corpses, he wouldn't, he's too afraid of . . .

THE WASHER/DOÑA ESTRELITA

'N' you bin Dame Dorothy Browne, his wife.
Please ta meetchoo. Now I taket him to da river fer his bath.
You bin right, he bin verra much afraidet. Help him ta die,
Missus, quench da fires dat sear him.

DAME DOROTHY

No! He doesn't . . . You're wrong.

THE WASHER/DOÑA ESTRELITA

Ast him yerself.

(Everyone looks at Browne again. He nods.)

DR. BROWNE

I sent for her; she's come. She knows what I want, can't you hear that?

DAME DOROTHY

Thomas. Not yet.

DR. BROWNE

I did not live well. That was true. I never intended harm. That was true.

DAME DOROTHY

You heard.

DR. BROWNE

Tell the children . . . No. Don't tell them anything.

(Dorothy leaves.)

DR. SCHADENFREUDE

Death's little cottage industries. Are you a vigorous scrubber?

THE WASHER/DOÑA ESTRELITA

Da skin glows where I scrubet; it blush 'n' glow.

DR. SCHADENFREUDE

When my time comes, will you scrub for me?

THE WASHER/DOÑA ESTRELITA

Someone will.

DR. SCHADENFREUDE

Thomas, enjoy your bath. Shall I have a servant carry him?

THE WASHER/DOÑA ESTRELITA

No need, I have strong arms.

(Schadenfreude leaves, smiling.
The Weaver gathers her things and starts to leave.

At the last minute she throws a little holy water on Browne and exits, muttering Latin.)

DR. BROWNE

(Wiping water off his face) The bath's already begun. How did I know you were coming to me? The ship, the warm seas . . .

THE WASHER/DOÑA ESTRELITA

Hush, don't try to understand.

DR. BROWNE

Across the wide, calm, bathwater sea, pearly pink or moon-dappled, you sailed to me, to my deathbed, how mysterious, with candle-flickering eyes and cool, pale arms . . .

THE WASHER/DOÑA ESTRELITA

You never understood, Thomas.

DR. BROWNE

I think now I never thought enough about love.

THE WASHER/DOÑA ESTRELITA

You never did. Come.

(She lifts him in her arms.)

THE WASHER/DOÑA ESTRELITA

Easy. To the river.

(They exit. His Soul sits up.)

HIS SOUL

(Sings:)
And do you love me, darling one?
To touch your face is lots of fun.

Your skin so clear and waist so trim:
"I cannot get enough of him!"
"I cannot get enough of her,
I want to eat the stuff of her!"
Ooh ah ooh ah,
The Heavens wheel and spin.
The Heavens wheel and spin.

And will you love me when I'm dead?
When hair and skin are off my head?
When bone is bared, and viscera,
Will you, my dear, still kisscera?
Oh will the little games we played
Still tempt us when we're both decayed?
Mortal love, mortal love,
Stabbed in the heart with mortal love.

Yesterday morn your breath was bad,
And truth to tell, it made me sad
To smell the hint upon that breath
Of the work of corruption
And the progress of Death.

(Intermission.)

Act Three

THE DANCE OF DEATH

Glorious Golden Country Sunshine, Late Afternoon

Browne's bed is empty, as at the end of Act Two.
Maccabbee enters, carrying a very swollen strangled Chicken C.

MACCABBEE

'Tis a new age a scientiftic wondrament. Hemprical hobservations 'n' da careful hexamination a seemingly insignifticant phenomenas. Who knows where it all leadet?

Dis chicken weighet three 'n' halfet pounds when it bin alive. Aftah death, it weighet eight pounds, like I told him. Now it weigh thirteen pounds. 'N' I suspeck 'n' predick it han't done haccumulating mass, neiver.

(He puts the strangled chicken on Browne's pillow) I leavet here 'n' he can see fer himself, when he bin finishet wif his baptism.

(Little pause)

I wanna die inna grand style, wif a sense of pompet 'n' circumfrence, but I bin probably gonna die hignominious, all loathesome 'n' wacket a da clap inna poorhouse hovel. He coulda hadda nicet kind a death, he got da money fer it, but he always bin knacky. Evah readet one a his books? I tried, oncet. I han't followet da narrative. Strucket me as hover-written.

(His Soul's voice is heard.)

HIS SOUL

You! Amanuensis! Hireling! Water boy!

MACCABBEE

A voicet! *(He turns around)* A disembloodet voicet! *Verra* creepet. Must be a hecho. *(Turns back)*

HIS SOUL

MACCABBEEEEEEEE!

(Maccabbee turns again. His Soul rises slowly.)

MACCABBEE

Wirret. A miniscule homunculus. Who you be, babbie, da toof fairy?

HIS SOUL

I'm . . . I'm Browne's soul.

MACCABBEE

Aw, hang dat up ta dry. You han't his soul. He han't got one.

HIS SOUL

He'd like to believe that, but here I am, a casualty of his crisis of faith.

MACCABBEE

Ef you bin da verra soul a Browne, how come you han't down by da rivah, watching him get washet by dat knacky old bat he sent fer?

HIS SOUL

I expected to go with him, like before, but there was only a tug. You . . . you see me.

MACCABBEE

Hobviously.

HIS SOUL

Something's wrong. He ought to be dead soon, and I should be well-nigh to weightless, but . . .
Touch me.

MACCABBEE

What fer?

HIS SOUL

Just . . . the tip of my finger. Just a quick touch.

(Maccabbee does it. His Soul draws back in horror and disgust.)

HIS SOUL

Oh God! How revolting!

MACCABBEE

Dat's a mighty shitten thing ta say. Han't you got manners?

HIS SOUL

Oh God you *touched* me. I've been *touched.*

MACCABBEE

Calm yerself, ya han't catch it just by touching.

HIS SOUL

Catch what?

MACCABBEE

Da clap.

HIS SOUL

The . . . ?
Oh God, I've become . . . *meat*. Oh god I have a *skin*. Oh, but that's imposs . . .
The *clap*. What's "*the clap*"?

MACCABBEE

A venereal hinfection. A disease constracted by fornicating hindiscriminately.

HIS SOUL

I feel sick.

MACCABBEE

Well how ya think I feel? It consumet my nose. It's a harful hembarrassment. Dis bronze prophylactus han't foolet no one, though it bin more decorative dan a wood one, don't ya think?

HIS SOUL

Kill him.

MACCABBEE

Secuse me?

HIS SOUL

Kill him! Browne! Kill kill kill him! He has to die soon! Look, look at me!

MACCABBEE

You look OK. A little wirret, but . . .

HIS SOUL

You shouldn't be able to look at me at all! I'm METAPHYSICAL! Three weeks ago even *he* couldn't see me, and now I'm being *fingered* by his manservant. I'm doomed unless he dies! I want to climb! Save me, kill the bastard—it's your duty as a Christian.

MACCABBEE

I dunno, dat be hard ta sell ta a judge 'n' jury.

HIS SOUL

I'll give you something.

MACCABBEE

Like what, fer instance?

HIS SOUL

Well, like . . . oh anything, WHATEVER, I don't care.

MACCABBEE

I'll do it if ya get inna bed with me.

HIS SOUL

If I do . . . *what*?

MACCABBEE

I han't ever made it with a metaphysical hactuality before.

HIS SOUL

I'll burn in Hell first.

MACCABBEE

Ah, yoop. Well, lemme think.
You bin going ta Heaven aftah he dies?

HIS SOUL

Yes! Heaven! If he dies soon!

MACCABBEE

When you arrivet in Heaven, talket to da Blesstet Virgin 'r someone with charitable hinclinations. Rid me a da clap. Bringet back my nose.

HIS SOUL

I couldn't . . . guarantee anything, of course, but I . . . might . . .

MACCABBEE

Ef ya gimme yer wordet, I kill him onna gamble.

HIS SOUL

You'd kill your master on a *gamble*?

MACCABBEE

It bin sumpin I always wannet ta do anyway. 'N' ef it gets me a miracleous restoration on my nose, so much da more da merrier, 'tis what I say.

HIS SOUL

Deal. But nothing painful, and . . . try not to enjoy it too much. *(Looking upward)* Forgive me, Father, I don't know what I'm doing. Well, I do know, but . . . Oh God, *skin, meat, blood*, oh help me, help me, I think I'm starting to . . . to *smell* . . .

(His Soul vanishes as Babbo enters, splotchy with various fruit jellies.)

BABBO

I bin distresset. I searchet through evah one a dem hot baket tarts, 'n' I hant find da one with dat papah. Maybe it burnet hup.

MACCABBEE

I gotta a remedy fer when things feelet upset-down.

BABBO

What?

(They look at each other.)

BABBO

Now?

MACCABBEE

'N' look! Da bed bin unoccupied.

BABBO

Ah, nope, not dere, da linens on dat bed bin soilet to da verra point a crawling.

MACCABBEE

It's da smella weariness 'n' fear. Maket me wanna do da Molloch.

BABBO

Probably a mordal sin . . . Ah, well, I gotta coupla minnits.

(They hop into bed and begin to fuck. Dame Dorothy enters, carrying a candle; Maccabbee throws the covers over them just in time and they lie very still, but Chicken C is left lying atop the bedclothes. Dorothy goes to the desk and begins searching through the papers. Maccabbee sits up, tosses Chicken C behind the headboard and goes back under the covers.)

DAME DOROTHY

Oh why bother searching? He obviously didn't write a Will. Punish the world for continuing after, keep everyone worrying until he's gone: it would be so like Thomas to die intestate.

(From her bodice she produces a document looking very much like the document Dr. Browne gave Babbo in Act One. She looks to make sure she's alone, then reads it, audibly, but to herself.)

DAME DOROTHY

"I Sir Thomas Browne being of sound mind etcetera etcetera etcetera do hereby bequeath etcetera etcetera all my shares in the Walsingham Quarry to my beloved wife Dame Dorothy etcetera . . ."

(She goes to Browne's desk, places the fake Will in the desk drawer. Pumpkin enters with a corpse wrapped in a shroud. She doesn't hear him. He drops the corpse on the floor near her. She spins, badly startled.)

PUMPKIN

Afternoon, Dorfy.

(She sees the corpse and screams.)

PUMPKIN

'Tis a client a mine.

DAME DOROTHY

Oh mercy, I thought it was Thomas.

PUMPKIN

Ah, nope, bin some poor old sot dey give me ta bury inna pauper's field. I bringet him to da German doctah in hexchange fer a nominous recompensideration.

(Dorothy bends close to the corpse to see it more clearly, holding her candle. When she gets too close, the candle flares wildly!! Dorothy jumps back.)

PUMPKIN

Could you put out dat candle, Dorfy?

(Dorothy blows out the candle.)

PUMPKIN

Thanks, da earfly remains a dis doof bin so fulla gin and cheap brandy combustiples a spark might hignite a hexplosion.

DAME DOROTHY

Could we . . . could you put him somewhere? Under the bed, or . . . it's unnerving.

PUMPKIN

Ah, yup. Secuset.

(He stows the corpse under the bed.)

PUMPKIN

A man gotta be henterprising. Han't catchet me passing by a chance ta supplement my yearning.

DAME DOROTHY

You're an ambitious man, Leonard.

PUMPKIN

You still bin broodet, my love.

DAME DOROTHY

I . . . I've made a difficult decision, Leonard. I have to tell you something.
(Little pause)
I am going to be the owner of the quarry, Leonard, when Thomas dies. Of the Walsingham fields, of the quarry, of this house and estate—

PUMPKIN

'N' a gross heapet horde inna bank.

DAME DOROTHY

Yes. I was looking for the Will, to make sure everything's in order, because . . . I have plans, Leonard.
When Thomas is dead, and a proper amount of time has passed, I want to marry you, Mr. Pumpkin.

PUMPKIN

Be Dorfy Pumpkin den, 'n' not a Dame 'r nuffin. But ef we growet rich enough dey might knight me someday.

DAME DOROTHY

And after we marry . . .
And then I intend to make Walsingham Fields common land again. Open to cottagers, smallholders.

PUMPKIN

For rent.

DAME DOROTHY

No rent. Free, common lands. Close down the quarry, let the grass grow over it, water fill it, cover the machines, the scars. In ten years time it will be as though it had never existed.

(Pause.)

PUMPKIN

Dorfy—

DAME DOROTHY

And you and I will have a cottage there, and live poor but happy existences growing what we need and praying to God for forgiveness. Oh, Leonard, I know you wanted wealth but believe me, I know what wealth is and—

PUMPKIN

You know what, Dorfy? You ent actually know nuffin. What dis about, huh? Bin a test ta see ef I lovet, ta see ef I be true without da money, bin dat?

DAME DOROTHY

No, Leonard, it's my . . . it's what I want, Leonard.

PUMPKIN

Well, den fuck whatchoo want, cause dat be da knackiest 'n' stupidest shit I ever sat 'n' listet to.

DAME DOROTHY

Leonard—

PUMPKIN

Common lands. Whatchoo know about dat? I bin a boy onna commons—I watchet teef fall out 'n' hair turn gray onna heads a da young. I seen da men 'n' wimmin actet like beasten, act like da dumb ox 'n' da beatet dog, crushet by da heavy hand a no idea what dere be in dis world, dat dere bin more ta hexistence dan birth 'n' grief 'n' bitter death. 'N' I see da rich go by in deir silk 'n' gold 'n' jewelet, like high dark angels dat inhabitet another earf, where you han't no hope cause you bin stucket inna common lands by Gawd. But I left. 'N' thanks fer da invitation, Dame Dor-o-fy, but I han't going back.

DAME DOROTHY

We could share. Make common cause with the other cottagers, like the ranters say.

PUMPKIN

Dere bin no more ranters, Dorfy. Dey bin squashet by da bishops years ago, 'n' dem three hoors ya taket in bin eiver deludet, 'r lying, 'r both. Oncet dere bin thousands rantet. 'N' shaket 'n' quaket 'n' level 'n' dig. Say no rent, say food from da heavens, 'n' even though I bin a boy den I knew it bin crap, bin fairy stories 'n' farts inna wind. 'N' now dem voicet ent heard from no more. We gotta get on with da bloodet business a making do. I digget graves fer da rich 'n' poor. Da rich pay better but I han't say which I enjoy da most ta dig. 'N' before dey dig a grave fer me, I gonna be rich. 'N' dat be with you, Dorfy, 'r not.
You throw out what most folks never had.

(Pause.)

DAME DOROTHY

Ten miles from here there is the highway. People sleep on the open road at night. On cold mornings there's some who don't wake up. You see them, ice-crusted . . . I want a thicker skin but it won't grow. At night I hear those machines in the quarry pounding and I think: it's flesh those hammers pound, it's bone. We're immensely rich but we live without luxury. He can't bear to part with anything, even remorse, and I can't bear the accumulation.

Thomas is lucky to die. I must live on here for a while yet, and I hate this life. In me there is a bleeding wound, and it never heals, and it's full of blood, and full of light, and there's paradise in there, besieged and unreachable but always beckoning. And the more foul and ugly the world becomes the more it beckons. The more it aches.
I can't live like this, Leonard, I have to do something.

PUMPKIN

When da doctah bin dead, Dorfy, 'n' I dug his grave . . . we talket summore. Do nuffin till den. Alright?
I love you, Dorfy.

DAME DOROTHY

Promise me, Leonard: tell my plans to no one. Promise.

PUMPKIN

Ah, yup. Come to da woods. I wanna soothe yer yeart.

DAME DOROTHY

My heart needs that.
Are you with me, Leonard?

PUMPKIN

Right now I be.

(They look at each other, then exit silently. Maccabbee sticks his head up, then Babbo.)

MACCABBEE

How about dat?

BABBO

Da missus bin swoggling da gravedigger.

MACCABBEE

Him dying maket her hotter 'n him living ever did.

BABBO

I wanna leavet. I gotta find dat tart . . .
(Hearing something) Hisst!

(They throw the covers over themselves again, as Dogwater enters. He looks about, making sure he's alone, then removes from an inner pocket a fake Will. He skim-reads.)

DR. DOGWATER

"I Sir Thomas B-B-Browne, being of sound mind and buh-body . . . do by this instrument deed all my shuh-shares in the Walsingham Quarry to Luh-Luh-Leviticus Duh-Dogwater, D. Duh-D. . . . In ah-appreciation of . . ." buh-buh-blah and so forth. We promise You, uh-Almighty God, we will cuh-continue to search every nuh-nook and cranny for the ruh-real Will, but . . . Fuh-forgive us our fuh-forgeries as we forgive those who fuh-fuh-forge against us.

(He puts the Will in the Bible, when suddenly he hears someone coming and runs to the bed. He almost dives under the bedclothes, then at the last minute he sniffs the linens and changes his mind, hiding instead behind the drapes.
The Weaver enters and begins to search through the papers on the desk. Dogwater jumps out and surprises her.)

DR. DOGWATER

It's a fuh-fuh-flogging offense at the very least, burglary.

THE WEAVER/THE ABBESS OF X

AH! Oh, oh please, Pastah, han't callet da authorities, I was only . . . uh . . . looking fer my needles. I lost dem in dis pile a papah.

DR. DOGWATER

Do you think I'm a fuh-fool? Your story is tuh-transparently false. You're a cuh-common thief and you nuh-need a good fuh-fuh-flogging. This way, please.

(He grabs her roughly by the arm. She executes a perfect karate flip and drops him to the floor.)

THE WEAVER/THE ABBESS OF X
Oops. Sorry, Pastah, dat was a hinvoluntary reflex.

DR. DOGWATER
(Scrambling to his feet) How duh-duh-dare you?

THE WEAVER/THE ABBESS OF X
(Dropping into a fighting stance) Ah, Pastah, han't be wise ta fight wif me, I bin verra dangerous.

DR. DOGWATER
(Circling in) Dangerous! The duh-day I'm unable to best an old crone in a test of phuh-physical prowess is the day I . . .

(She lunges, jabs him sharply in the guts, spins, chops him in the neck, and kicks him in the ass. He goes sprawling.)

THE WEAVER/THE ABBESS OF X
I warnet you.

DR. DOGWATER
You're nuh-no shuh-shroud weaver.

(Pause.)

THE WEAVER/THE ABBESS OF X
No.

DR. DOGWATER
In the nuh-name of God, who are you?

THE WEAVER/THE ABBESS OF X
I bin someone you knew verra well, oncet.

DR. DOGWATER

I thought you were familiar. Who . . .

(She removes her disguise.)

THE ABBESS OF X

Hello, Leviticus.

DR. DOGWATER

Ah, nuh-no, it cuh-cuh-can't be y . . .
Ah-ah-ah-ah—

THE ABBESS OF X

Alice.

DR. DOGWATER

Then where have you buh-been, oh Alice, where have—

THE ABBESS OF X

I was almost your bride once, Leviticus. A long time ago. Now you see me, a bride of Christ.

DR. DOGWATER

A wh . . . ? A *nah-nah-nah-NUN*?!

THE ABBESS OF X

An abbess.

DR. DOGWATER

A cah-cah-Catholic nah-nah-nah—

THE ABBESS OF X

Ave Maria, Leviticus, et pax vobiscum.

DR. DOGWATER

When you d . . . d . . . Alice, when the shipwreck, when I huh-heard, I was inconsolable, Alice. I foreswore puh-pleasure and my thoughts turned Heavenward, for suh-suh-suh—

THE ABBESS OF X

For succor.

DR. DOGWATER

In your memory I dedicated my life to His service. And in God I found suh-sweetness surpassing, but only by a luh-little, the sweetness I'd known with you.
And now God torments me by returning you to me, a muh-minion of the antichrist in ruh-Rome, a rag of the buh-buh-beast.

THE ABBESS OF X

The One True Church. And you, Leviticus, a lieutenant schismatic.

DR. DOGWATER

It's a good thing I'm not disposed to despair. I assume, Alice, that as a nah-nun, you now subscribe to the uh-unnatural puh-practice of celibacy?

THE ABBESS OF X

I must request that you cease to address me by my former name. Alice Browne perished in that shipwreck. In Christ's Church she was reborn, and by His vicar on earth she was rebaptised.

DR. DOGWATER

And to what name does she cuh-currently answer?

THE ABBESS OF X

Mother Magdalena Vindicta, of the Abbey of X.

DR. DOGWATER

Aix-en-Provence? Puh-pretty town, I vuh-visited it once in my travels.

THE ABBESS OF X

No, not Aix. X. The Abbey of X.

DR. DOGWATER

I suh-said Aix.

THE ABBESS OF X

Not A-I-X. Just X.

DR. DOGWATER

X.

THE ABBESS OF X

Just . . . *X.*

DR. DOGWATER

And where, pray tell, is that?

THE ABBESS OF X

I'm not at liberty to say.

In the first flush of my newfound faith I joined the Discalced Carmelites, but I found them too French, not strict enough. Then over the years I learned of other British nuns, expatriates, and we banded together—the sole survivors of our fatherland's spiritual collapse.

DR. DOGWATER

I object to that.

THE ABBESS OF X

We laughed and wept as God smote your Apostasy with pestilence worse than the Egyptian plagues. And finally we decided to take a hand . . .

DR. DOGWATER

A hand in what?

THE ABBESS OF X

We trained for years in Sicily. The bloody arts, unfit, some might say, for women: violence, poison and war. And we became adepts. Of great precision and skill.

DR. DOGWATER

Wh-what are you tuh-talking about?

THE ABBESS OF X

The death of Cromwell, for example.

DR. DOGWATER

A nuh-natural death.

THE ABBESS OF X

If you call belladonna natural, yes.

DR. DOGWATER

Are you suh-saying that you ah-assassinated Cuh-Cromwell?

THE ABBESS OF X

My predecessor did. And the last two archbishops of Canterbury. We have their hats hanging on the wall of our refectory.

DR. DOGWATER

Thuh-this is monstrous. I don't believe you.

THE ABBESS OF X

We will not rest until we've driven the last vestiges of the False Creed out of England.

DR. DOGWATER

And you ruh-really expect to do that? One little cuh-convent full of addled nuns?

THE ABBESS OF X

It's a beginning.

DR. DOGWATER

Y-you're completely insane, Alice. The Church of England is the Church of the fuh-fuh-future. No one wants Cah-Catholicism back. We duh-don't sell indulgences now, we sell cuh-cuh-commodities! The tide of history—

THE ABBESS OF X

God's truth knows no history! The Mysteries of the Faith aren't subservient to market fluctuations! A true servant of Christ is not shaken by surface changes in worldly affairs. We are entering a time of great tribulation when men strive to have pierced the Cloud of Unknowing, to have stripped the veil from the face of God. And what horrors will that not unleash? But the Church, Leviticus, is built on a rock and will withstand the firestorm, while your wretched and compromised adaptation stands only on a shifting pile of cash—and the winds will scatter it, the whole ragbag scrapheap.

DR. DOGWATER

God will dispose of us as He sees fit, and adaptability is His wuh-way. With a buh-breath of his nostrils He suh-swept away your cloud, and let me tell you suh-something, Alice, nuh-no one misses it. We want light, not dah-dah-darkness. Plain words, not Luh-Latin blather. Your priests are fuh-fat. I'm not fuh-fat. I don't buh-bathe my flesh in wine and milk, I suh-swim in fuh-freezing ponds. Harsh, but solid! My faith has an industrial vitality. Work for Christ! Accumulate! Accumulate! That's my cuh-credo!

THE ABBESS OF X

They should never have translated the Bible. You are the crippled progeny of that labor.

DR. DOGWATER

Why did you come back?

THE ABBESS OF X

My brother will die a Catholic.

DR. DOGWATER

Over my d . . . over my d . . . my d . . . like Hell he will. He's a puh-professed Protestant.

THE ABBESS OF X

A mere technicality.

DR. DOGWATER

If his soul is all you're concerned about, why are you ruh-rifling through his thuh-things? Luh-looking for something? Puh-perhaps the luh-last Will and Testament. Perhaps not so unconcerned with muh-money after all.

THE ABBESS OF X

Our abbey needs funds, Leviticus. An endowment would be a blessing, spare us from soliciting contributions through . . . other methods.

DR. DOGWATER

I shall reveal this to Thomas when he returns.

THE ABBESS OF X

You loved me once.

DR. DOGWATER

Wuh-once I did. But the woman I loved is d . . .

THE ABBESS OF X

Dead. Then we are enemies.

DR. DOGWATER

Unalterably and uh-irrevocably. Your buh-brother will suh-spurn you, you won't get a cent.

THE ABBESS OF X

We'll see.
He was never one of you. He's not so well scrubbed. His books are very strange.

DR. DOGWATER

I nuh-never liked them. But at heart, Thomas is suh-suh-solid. A buh-business-minded man. A suh-scientist.

THE ABBESS OF X

A scientist. When we were children, he tried to learn to track and plot the stars. Maps, charts, astronomy, a new science. But night after night he would sit in the grass and gaze up at the sky, mouth and eyes wide open, and shiver at the immensity, the immeasurability, the profound depth of Heaven. The charts lay idle, soaking up the night dew gathering in the grass. He was never a scientist.
He'll help his sister. I shall pray for it.

DR. DOGWATER

Puh-pray all you like! God's fuh-forgotten Latin! He won't understand a wuh-word!

(She begins to exit, then suddenly performs another spectacular martial arts maneuver, knocking Dogwater flat. She pulls a fake Will from her wimple, stuffs it under the pillow on the bed, gathers up her disguise and exits.)

DR. DOGWATER

(Still flat out, in pain) Was that ruh-really necessary?

(Maccabbee sneaks out of the bed and exits. Schadenfreude enters. Schadenfreude watches Babbo, who is sneaking out of bed. She exits as Dogwater, unseeing, from the floor, says:)

DR. DOGWATER

(Rising, wincing in pain, not seeing yet that the Abbess is gone) You wuh-wrenched my back!

(Dogwater limps to the family Bible to check on his Will.)

DR. SCHADENFREUDE

(Gleeful) Searching for lost souls, perhaps?

(Dogwater turns, startled.)

DR. SCHADENFREUDE

Find the Will yet?

DR. DOGWATER

That duh-doesn't concern you.

DR. SCHADENFREUDE

It does. I want to be Sir Thomas's eulogist. It's only fitting: we were both men of science, I stewarded him through his final illness and did it well, regardless of your low opinion of my procedures. It means a lot to me.

DR. DOGWATER

I have a nagging suspicion you aren't muh-motivated exclusively by fah-fah-fraternal affections.

DR. SCHADENFREUDE

His Majesty the King will be in attendance at the funeral.

DR. DOGWATER

I nuh-know. What can that puh-possibly mean to you?

DR. SCHADENFREUDE

The office of Court Physician, I hear, is open.

DR. DOGWATER

I duh-doubt that they'll want the position fuh-filled by a juh-German. No offense.

DR. SCHADENFREUDE

(Smiling, happy) None taken. I have a letter of recommendation to the king from his cousin the elector of Hanover.

DR. DOGWATER

Then why don't you just guh-go to Luh-London with your letter? What are you duh-doing here?

DR. SCHADENFREUDE

I arrived in London in 1649, precisely on the day of Charles the First's decapitation. A king without a head . . .

DR. DOGWATER

Duh-doesn't need a doctor.

DR. SCHADENFREUDE

(Amused) JA! I settled here, in Norfolk, where I could be inconspicuous.

(Dogwater gives him a look.)

DR. SCHADENFREUDE

And now with the crown secure on the royal head and the royal head secure on the rest of the royal body my desire to serve His Majesty prompts me forward. What better way to make an impression than with a gripping eulogy for a highly esteemed artist and monarchist? It's the least I'm owed for my services.

DR. DOGWATER

Dr. Schadenfreude, I am the puh-prelate for this parish, and huh-highly trained, and I will give the eulogy. You'll have to look elsewhere for a ruh-rostrum for your tuh-tuh-tawdry political mah-mah-machinations.

(Schadenfreude pulls off a glove and slaps Dogwater!)

DR. SCHADENFREUDE

(Echt Prussian!) Dogwater, I challenge you to a duel.

DR. DOGWATER

A duel? You expect a man of God to fuh-fight a duel?

DR. SCHADENFREUDE

(Wielding his walking stick like a fencing foil) JA! Of *words*! Your eulogy against mine! Let each applicant for the position commit his text to memory! And then let Browne decide!

(Dogwater shakes the end of the walking stick, which has been pointed at his chest, in grim agreement.
The Washer enters, carrying Browne wrapped in a blanket.)

DR. DOGWATER

Huh-he's buh-back.

(She places him in the bed.)

DR. SCHADENFREUDE

Did he enjoy his bath? Or did it kill him?

THE WASHER/DOÑA ESTRELITA

Bin livet still, but bin verra close to da end.

DR. DOGWATER

Buh-Browne? Can you hear me? The Will, Browne, the Wuh-Will!

DR. BROWNE

(Deep in a blissful, sexy dream) . . . in tunnels underneath . . .

DR. DOGWATER

Tuh-tunnels?

DR. BROWNE

. . . buried deep . . .

DR. DOGWATER

The Will? You buh-buried the Will?

DR. BROWNE

Yes. By the river. Deep.

DR. DOGWATER

He buh-buried it! By the rah-river! Oh God, I am beset from all suh-sides. Where can I get a shovel?

(He rushes out.)

DR. BROWNE

(Luscious, sensual, happy) Tunnels by the river. Large, black velvet, muscular moles. With formidable claws and paddle paws and tough little cartilage-blunt stubbins for noses, blind blind blind blind blind . . .
Estrelita?

DR. SCHADENFREUDE

Estrelita?

DR. BROWNE

Doña Estrelita . . .

(He sinks entirely into sleep.)

DR. SCHADENFREUDE

Who is Doña Estrelita, Browne?

(Doña Estrelita sheds her disguise; under her weaver rags and mask she is a spectacular Spanish noblewoman, dressed to the nines.)

DOÑA ESTRELITA

I am.

DR. SCHADENFREUDE

And who are you? Really?

DOÑA ESTRELITA

Doña Estrelita Maria Luz Angelica Brava y Gambon. The wife of the Spanish ambassador to the court of Charles II.

DR. SCHADENFREUDE

You're the wife of the Sp . . . and this washing business, something you do for a lark?

DOÑA ESTRELITA

A small deception to gain access.
Decades ago I loved this man. No one knows how much.
I've come to help him die. And take him home, to Spain, with me.

DR. SCHADENFREUDE

To Spain?

DOÑA ESTRELITA

I can't bear the thought of him resting in this swampsoil, dissolving. Years ago I gave him up to the suction of this marshy island. In death, at last, I will have him with me, in the crucible land, the desert land of sand and dry ash, in Spain.

DR. SCHADENFREUDE

I'm flattered that you chose to reveal yourself to me, great lady.

DOÑA ESTRELITA

Fellow foreigner.

DR. SCHADENFREUDE

I am a student of the world's variety and I have observed . . . There are many kinds of lovers. Some sunlit and happy. Some moonstruck and griefstricken.

DOÑA ESTRELITA

And some driven by curious passions, pallid, silent, drawn to the dark.

(They stare at each other with an icy fervor.)

DR. SCHADENFREUDE

We are, I suspect, kindred spirits, Doña.

DOÑA ESTRELITA

You are from the cold north, Doctor. I am from the hot south. It's the people in the middle I don't trust.

DR. SCHADENFREUDE

And how, most charming lady, do you plan to accomplish this crypt robbing? You won't get him out the front door.

DOÑA ESTRELITA

(Hearing a noise) Someone's coming! My disguise!

(Maccabbee enters, carrying a huge urn. Estrelita hides in the curtains.)

MACCABBEE

Da urn arrivet. Bin dead?

DR. SCHADENFREUDE

What have we here?

(Schadenfreude examines the urn, Maccabbee goes to the bed. His Soul appears.)

HIS SOUL

You have to do it soon! I've become so *thick*!

MACCABBEE

My nose, remembah!

HIS SOUL

SOON!

MACCABBEE

(Searching the bedclothes) You seen dat chicken, Doctah Schadenfreude?

(His Soul reaches behind the headboard and throws Maccabbee the chicken, swollen even larger than at the top of the scene. His Soul sinks from view.)

MACCABBEE

Here 'tis. Gawd, I gotta weigh dis bird again. It bin positively collostal.

(He goes with the chicken.)

DR. SCHADENFREUDE

He's gone.
Doña Estrelita, he's gone.
Dona Estrelita?

(She crawls out.)

DOÑA ESTRELITA

(Delighted) There's a body under this bed.

DR. SCHADENFREUDE

(Looking) A spare! Redolent of Barbados rum!

DOÑA ESTRELITA

Is there a large oven in the house?

DR. SCHADENFREUDE

In the kitchen.

DOÑA ESTRELITA

I want to have a look. I gotta plan.

(They exit.
Death enters, eating a tart. He bites down on something unexpected and removes from the tart Dr. Browne's Will. Placing the tart on Browne's bed, Death opens it, reads and chuckles.)

DEATH

(Striking a pose for declaming poetry, one foot forward, one hand behind his back:)
Unsound, thy body;
unstrung, thy mind,
and yet thou leave'st thy Will behind.

(He pockets the Will. He raises his knife, walks toward Browne, ready to kill, then stops, uncertain.
Sarah enters.)

DEATH

I'm very . . . unhappy.

SARAH

Hoosh, babbie, I knowet.

DEATH

It's like sharp nettles. I frighten him. He doesn't love me. I want his love. I want to rip his heart out and eat it. *(He raises his knife to strike)*

SARAH

Soon, babbie, soon . . . I gotta little do ta do, firstet.

(Death moves a step or two toward Sarah. She is very frightened of him, but holds her ground.)

DEATH

It's the appetite that never dies. The body dies. The mind dies. The heart stops beating. EVERYTHING DROPS AWAY! But this sharp painful hunger lingers on.

SARAH

Dancet wif me, babbie. It taket yer mind off da ache.

(Death approaches her, she backs away at first, involuntarily recoiling from him. Then she takes his proffered hand. They dance slowly as His Soul sings.)

HIS SOUL

(Singing:)
The lamb of God is bleating,
Heaven help the stupid thing!

For the daylight is retreating
And the owl is on the wing.

On the wing the hungry owl;
There is murder on the wind;
And the wolf is on the prowl;
And a scent is in the air . . .

A bloody teardrop rolling
From its gold reproachful eye:
Thou hast I think forsook thy lamb
And no more hear its cry:

Crying pity and despair;
For a scent is in the air;
And there's murder in the wind;
And the wolf is on the prowl;
Oh forgive me, I have sinned;
On the wing, the hungry owl . . .

(The other ranters enter. Death bows, Sarah curtsies. He kisses her hand and leaves. As the song concludes the ranters surround Browne's bed.)

HIS SOUL

Ah, faith.
It is amazing.
And the night is dark and chill,
And the little lamb is grazing
On a clover-covered hill.
And the stars are blotted out
By the cold and distant moon
And the night grows darker still;
Pray for daybreak.
Make it soon.

(Intermission.)

Act Four

WHO SEES GOD'S FACE, THAT IS SELF LIFE, MUST DIE

Fiery Apocalyptic Sunset, Early Evening

Browne is alone, sleeping on his bed. The ranters surround him, watching.
Sarah makes a gesture and the lights in the room dim and change.

SARAH

Dere bin always a time a reckoning, Browne, a counting a da stores 'n' a parceling out, 'n' dat time come fer you at last.
'Tis now fer da rant 'n' da curset, fellow creatures. Helpet 'n' make dis loafa bad bread ready fer da doings, whilst I preparet myself.

(Sarah undresses. Mary and Ruth undress Browne and hoist him, unconscious, to his feet. Browne and Sarah stand nude together.)

RUTH

(Looking at them naked) Gawd bless my peeps, 'tis religious art! Hadam 'n' Heve inna Garden a Heden!

MARY

What happent to da snaket?

SARAH

Da serpent hiss 'n' slitheret, 'n' tell lies, 'n' wigglet 'n' flap, 'n' lead all astray.

(She pries open Browne's mouth and grabs his tongue.)

SARAH

Here bin da serpent tempter, 'n' now dis picture bin completet. 'Tis time. Ruth. Commencet da rant.

RUTH

(A prayer) Dere han't much comfort here tonight, but han't ever been much a dat anywhere, since da world inceptet. What comfort, fellow creatures, they give to da dying Christ? Vinegar sponges 'n' spears.

(There's a delicate penny whistle, unseen, playing a sweet air. All three ranters look up, look at one another, smile. Sarah nods and Ruth looks at Mary. They breathe in unison, loud, twice. Mary has a drum, and she strikes two strong beats. Ruth begins. As the rant builds in intensity, the three women begin to dance, pulling powerful forces from the earth and raising them into the air. Lights and strange sounds, drums, voices, singing, the quarry engine. Magic is being done.)

RUTH

I gotta dig,
Gotta dig to da place,
Gotta sink to da place,

To da place a da pain,
To da place a da plain
To da plain a da bone,
To da mouf a complaint,
To da voicet screamet,
To da tongue, to da place,
To da verra verra place,
To da rivah say
NO!
To dis weepet,
Say NO!
To dis sorra,
Say
GAWD, OH GAWD, OH YISROEL 'N' JUDAH!
To da pain 'n' da grief
To da poor da believers
Bya sweat a da Lord
By da calloused hands a Christ
By da breath, by da blood,
By da bloody tears a Christ
By da wrinkled hands a Mary
'N' da stripet socks a Joseph
'N' DA GLORY HALLEJULAH
'N' DA ANGELS ALLA BLUE!
Like flies dey buzzet
Like da buzzet a da flies
Like da lamb
Like da ram
Like da bitter bite a wine
Like da blood inna mouth
Like da bush inna fire
'N' da curse
'N' da curse
'N' da curse
'N' da curse

MARY

(Overlaps starting with Ruth's "ANGELS ALLA BLUE" above:)
'N' da earf gonna freezet
'N' da earf gonna crack
'N' da earf go all blacket
'N' da earf
'N' da earf
'N' da watahs a da ocean
'N' da boiling a da sea
'N' da curse, 'n' da hand
'N' da curse, 'n' da dreadet . . .

(Sarah has now mounted Browne, riding piggyback, triumphant, as Ruth leads him in a small circle.)

MARY

'N' DERE GO DA CALLET GLORY!
'N' DERE GO DA CALLET SELAH!
'N' DERE GO DA DEVIL ARMET!
'N' DERE GO DA PITCH 'N' THUNDAH!
'N' da curse bin come
'N' dah curse bin come . . .

(From Browne's mouth a wild animal bray—one long raw note. Suddenly from the air above, mighty trumpets play the notes of the Dies Irae, *E Flat, D, E Flat, C, D, B Flat, C, C. All the other noise ceases, Browne slumps to the floor, and the ranters look toward the sound, awestruck. They have ranted many times, and have made magic before, but this is different . . .)*

RUTH

(Softly) 'N' den dere bin a stillet in da passes a da moon . . .

SARAH

(Softly) Selah. Selah. Oh Yisroel 'n' Judah. 'Tis da power a Gawd, oh hallelujah . . .

(The room is transformed, through lights, into a verdant green bower in a woods.)

SARAH

(Gentle) Cross dat stream, fellow creatures, inta dat little woods, bin home . . .
'N' da leaves sparkle, it bin spring, 'n' tendah, 'n' da light bin silvah, 'n' da tree bark black, 'n' da leaves dat particala shade a green, 'n', Oh, we remembah, 'n', Oh, we be back dere someday, 'n' in dis walk a exile we weepet, 'n' remembah da woods . . .

(She reaches with great sudden violence toward the heavens. A hot white light, obliterating all other light, breaks down upon her, and upon Browne at her feet.)

SARAH

(Rage) 'N' pour, let us pour into dis memory, fellow creatures, such . . . strong . . . *hate.*

(All three place their hands on Browne. Browne shudders and cries. From the fields outside, a deep, ominous earthquake rumble.)

SARAH

Dat bin enough. 'Tis done, 'n' will unfold in time.
Dr. Browne, I give you dis, dis one last gift, whatchoo give to my ma:
Dat you bin wide awake when da little gentleman come. 'N' he bin coming.

(They dress him and lay him back in the bed. Sarah puts her clothes on.)

MARY

Nicet rant, Ruth.

RUTH

(Loading up with silver again) I bin hinspired. Da curse take, Sarah?

(Sarah listens. Outside, the rumble rumbles again, fainter.)

SARAH

Oh, yoop.

(They exit.
Dr. Dogwater sneaks in, goes to the Bible, takes out his fake Will, produces a pencil, and speaking as writes:)

DR. DOGWATER

". . . and I further stipulate that Dr. Dogwater *alone* duh-deliver my eulogy, that nuh-*no* other puh- persons be allowed to suh-speak at my fuh-funeral *particularly* not my uh-overpriced fancy foreign physician whose cuh-cuh-criminal ineptitude in muh-medicinal matters is matched by his guh-guttural Tuh-Teutonic-ally inflected muh-muh-murder of the kuh-king's English."

(He kisses the Will, replaces it, exits.
Immediately upon his exit the Abbess of X, who has been hiding in the curtains, goes to the Bible, and removes Dogwater's Will. She takes from her robes a strange-looking device with a crank handle. She inserts the Will in a slot at the top of the device, cranks the handle, and opens a little drawer at the base of the gadget: the Will has been shredded into long strips. She puts the strips back in the Bible, checks under the mattress to makes sure her *Will is still there; she kisses it, makes the sign of the cross over her sleeping brother and leaves.*
Dorothy sneaks out from behind another curtain, replaces the Abbess's Will under the mattress with her own from the desk, strikes a match, sets the Abbess's Will afire. She hears someone coming. Dorothy ducks back behind the curtain, dropping the flaming Will, in a panic abandoning it on the floor by the bed, smoldering.
Babbo enters, looking for something. Then she spots the tart Death left on the bed. She claps her hands, picks it up, sticks first one hand and then another hand in the tart and starts to rifle its filling, smearing herself with purple goo. She scratches her head in confu-

sion, then sees Dorothy's Will on the floor. Babbo claps her hands again—she's found the Will—she retrieves it and stuffs it in the tart. She begins to leave with the tart, when Dorothy steps out from behind the curtain. She looks on the floor; the Will she dropped is gone. She looks at Babbo.)

DAME DOROTHY

Where's the . . .

BABBO

Where da what?

DAME DOROTHY

What's in that tart?

BABBO

(Hiding the tart behind her back) Han't see no tart.

DAME DOROTHY

Babbo, give me that tart.

(Babbo bolts from the room.)

DAME DOROTHY

Babbo! Give me that tart! Babbo!

(She exits in pursuit. Browne moans in his sleep; he wakes up.)

DR. BROWNE

Washed. All washed . . . Up.
Unspool, unclench, I will plant this onion in the earth . . .
And go on living . . .

(He strains to push the blockage out. He is stricken by another searing, tearing pain in his gut. He screams, clutches his side. He opens his eyes again and sees the urn.)

DR. BROWNE

You've arrived. Silent urn. Still mouth.
I remember the Capuchin catacombs in Rome. That quiet, that fragile stillness. Those dry, deflated bodies. The disappointed faces of the dead.

(Maccabbee enters with Chicken C, dragging it by its neck; it has swelled even more than when we last saw it—a medicine ball of a chicken; HUGE.
His Soul rises up behind the headboard in silent homicidal expectation.)

MACCABBEE

Doctah?

DR. BROWNE

Go fetch the gravedigger. The urn's arrived.

MACCABBEE

Looket. Da chicken. It bin heavier now dan before. Forty-seven pounds.

DR. BROWNE

(Lying back, closing his eyes) Monstrous fowl. And what do you conclude, Maccabbee?

MACCABBEE

I conclude dat death been fulla surpriset.

(Maccabbee swings the immense heavy chicken back over his head, intending to crush Browne with it; he swings too hard and the force of its parabola carries Maccabbee backward to the floor with a crash. Browne sits up, looks at Maccabbee on the floor.)

MACCABBEE

Oops. I slippet.

(Babbo enters. His Soul sinks from view.)

BABBO

Doctah, dere bin someone here ta see you. She wannet me ta prepare ya fer da shock.

DR. BROWNE

Maccabbee, go get the gravedigger. Wait. The urn. Unscrew the lid.

(Maccabbee does.)

DR. BROWNE

What's inside?

MACCABBEE

(Head in the urn; his words echo spookily as if being spoken into a deep well [use a microphone]) Noot but ashy stoof, dead gray sandy grit 'n' bit a bone.

DR. BROWNE

From which you conclude?

MACCABBEE

(Raising his head out of the urn) Nuffin.

DR. BROWNE

(Quiet despair) Exactly so.
(Fury) Where's that gravedigger, you idiot?

MACCABBEE

Inna woods wif yer wife.

(He exits.)

DR. BROWNE

Actually, I knew that.

BABBO

Doctah, yer visitah.

DR. BROWNE

Is it Alice?

BABBO

How you know dat?

DR. BROWNE

I saw her. Has she . . . Is she some sort of nun?

BABBO

Some sort, but I han't say what.

DR. BROWNE

Show her in.

(Babbo exits.)

DR. BROWNE

Oh open urn, cough up that dust.

(A spume of dust rises from the urn. Browne is badly startled, frightened, then:)

DR. BROWNE

See? The dead do rise.

(The Abbess enters.)

DR. BROWNE

(Finds her presence, the sight of her, frightening) Alice.

THE ABBESS OF X

You look well, Thomas.

DR. BROWNE

(Attempting politeness) And you, I must say, look ferocious.
(Almost afraid to ask) Is *he* here, too?

THE ABBESS OF X

Who, Thomas?

DR. BROWNE

But no, I suppose he couldn't be.
The silk merchant.

THE ABBESS OF X

Father?

DR. BROWNE

Does convent life agree with you, Alice? Not too quiet?

THE ABBESS OF X

It is an active order.

DR. BROWNE

I'm glad you didn't drown, that's damp.
Into the sea poor Alice was tossed.
Everyone thought that her life was done.
Blankety-blankety she wasn't lost.
She went in a sinner and came out a nun.

THE ABBESS OF X

(Moving toward the bed) Thomas, I must talk seriously with you, I—

DR. BROWNE

(Stopping her approach) The silk merchant Browne. He died . . . You never knew him, really. He died when I was eight. He was a granite-hearted drunkard, his sheets were soiled and stank like these. Father Dead.

THE ABBESS OF X

Thomas, I need to—

DR. BROWNE

(Turning away from her, trying to stop her from talking, frightened) My writing desk was once set up facing the window. In the daytime, the view of the fields, the weather and light. But at night, Alice, the window went black, a mirror; I could see nothing in it but my tired face, the little candle light, and sometimes, stranger things. The faces of the dead in the window at night. My children's faces. Father's. Waiting and hungry . . .
I moved the desk to face the wall. Eventually.

THE ABBESS OF X

Is there a Will, Thomas? Where's the Will? He was my father too, some of the money—

DR. BROWNE

(Stopping her) Alice *(Very fast)* I've had fourteen children with Dorothy; eight died in infancy; those are the ones I love. The others grew large and difficult. I wrote a few books; they knighted me for that, and because I stayed loyal to the king. I was wrong to support him, they were right to chop his head off, progress is inexorable and his blood greased the works. Now I'm dying, and you're a nun, how funny, with many a jolly tale to tell, no doubt, but it's been twenty years and I mourned your death once and I'm more comfortable now thinking you still dead, so please, whoever you are, go away. Your presence is too vital and it causes pain.

(Pause.)

THE ABBESS OF X

(Placing the vial of holy water on his pillow) Water from the Vatican—holy water. Do with it what you will.

Some of the money should go to me, Thomas, it was my birthright, too. Father's inheritance.

DR. BROWNE

There's a distinctly mercenary scent in the air tonight. This isn't me dying; it's a great deal of money rolling over.

THE ABBESS OF X

Am I named in the Will?

DR. BROWNE

(Suddenly desperate) Help me, Alice. I CAN'T SHIT.

THE ABBESS OF X

Neither could Father, after he took ill. You're fifty years old. So was he. You've inherited everything, even his death.
Good-bye.

(She goes. Browne drinks the holy water, greedily.
Maccabbee enters with a machete. His Soul sits up again to watch. Maccabbee sneaks up behind Browne, and then swings the machete mightily back over his head, screaming:)

MACCABBEE

AAAAAAAAAAAAAAAAAAAAAAAAAAAAAAHHH!

(Again swings too hard; the tip of the machete impales itself in the floor behind him. Browne looks over at Maccabbee, who fakes a sneeze.)

MACCABBEE

Choo!

(Babbo enters again. His Soul sinks from view.)

BABBO

Secuset da interruptet, but now dere bin another woman ta see you, verra helegant 'n' mystrous. I think she bin foreign; she talket funny.

(Dorothy enters.)

DR. BROWNE

Not so foreign after all.

BABBO

No, Doctah, dis han't da foreign woman, dis yer wife.

(Babbo goes.)

DAME DOROTHY

Thomas, there's a woman from court come to pay her respects. The wife of the Spanish ambassador. You never told me to expect . . .

DR. BROWNE

Expect anything and everything. Death is full of surprises, right, Maccabbee?

MACCABBEE

Fulla interruptet, too.

DAME DOROTHY

What are you doing with that cleaver?

MACCABBEE

Bin trimmet da shrubbery.

DAME DOROTHY

There's no shrubbery in here.

MACCABBEE

'Tis good ta be preparet. Ya nevah know where da odd bush pop up. Now secuse me, I gotta go cut da heads offa da rose bushes.

DR. BROWNE

Keep your eyes to the ground!

MACCABBEE

Right! Da moles!

DR. BROWNE

The moles.

MACCABBEE

Ef I see one, Doctah, I chop it in two.

DR. BROWNE

That's the spirit.

(Maccabbee goes.)

DR. BROWNE

Where is my Spanish guest?

DAME DOROTHY

I asked her to wait a moment. Thomas, the gravedigger's come . . . uh, he's *here*. Here's the gravedigger. Mr. Pumpkin.

(Dorothy opens the door. Pumpkin enters.
Browne glares at Pumpkin a beat, then:)

DR. BROWNE

Oh, good. I can't say I've been looking forward to this, Mr. Pumpkin, but I recognize a grave necessity.
Leave us, Dorothy.

DAME DOROTHY

Leave? Why?

DR. BROWNE

A man's interment is an intimate matter. Join the others. Search for the Will. I can hear them now, dismantling the library.

DAME DOROTHY

You want to hurt me, Thomas.

DR. BROWNE

I used to, very much. And I believe I did, on occassion.

DAME DOROTHY

More than once.

DR. BROWNE

I'll be dead. You can remarry.

DAME DOROTHY

I don't care about the Will. I want nothing from you.

DR. BROWNE

Then you won't be disappointed.

(Dorothy goes. Browne watches her leave and then:)

DR. BROWNE

She's a good person. Too good. No judgment. None at all. I mean, look who she married. See my point?

PUMPKIN

Yes, sir. I do.

(Little pause.)

DR. BROWNE

(Glaring at Pumpkin, trying to make him squirm) I want to be buried deep. Very deep but . . . not too deep. Apart from the mob, but not in a lonely place. Avoid the usual clichés—no willow trees, though I'd like a view, for summer evenings. No pine box. Flimsy. Use that urn. Toss out the previous occupant, or better yet, throw me in there with him and let us mingle. *(Little pause)* No markers, or, well, maybe just a little unpretentious stone. Maybe . . . "Here lies Sir Thomas Browne, scientist." "Here lies Sir Thomas Browne, who made his wife miserable." "Here lies Sir Thomas Browne, no grandchildren . . . BUT A GENIUS! SHAKESPEARE HAD NOTHING ON HIM!" *(He is now bellowing at Pumpkin with wild hatred and immense pride)* Or maybe an obelisk! Or a pyramid! A pyre! A *sea* burial, or . . . *GET OUT OF HERE!*

PUMPKIN

I han't following dis, Dr. Browne.

DR. BROWNE

(Great delirious newfound certainty!) *I* don't need *you*, wretch! I'M NOT GOING TO DIE. It isn't . . . *conceivable!* I can't . . . *IMAGINE* it.
IF I DIE . . . THE WORLD ENDS! And . . . *(The certainty is dissipating, the hatred of Pumpkin remains)* And we'll have no need of gravediggers then.

PUMPKIN

Ef dat happens, Dr. Browne, I findet another job. I bin verra . . .

DR. BROWNE

Flexible? Jack of all trades? Descendant of a sturdy race?

PUMPKIN

I bin dat fer sure.

DR. BROWNE

Ambitious.

PUMPKIN

Verra.

DR. BROWNE

Tell her I died *knowing*.
No, don't tell her anything.
I daresay you'll end up running the whole works one day.

(Dorothy enters.)

PUMPKIN

Da works.
Dr. Browne. Mrs. Browne.

(He strides out, triumphant.)

DR. BROWNE

I don't trust that boy, Dorothy. He's tense.

DAME DOROTHY

But dependable.

DR. BROWNE

Don't hate me, wife.

DAME DOROTHY

You did not live well upon this earth, Thomas. I never really wanted anything from you. And you leave behind you only a dreadful lot of woe.

(She goes.)

DR. BROWNE

(Considers that for a moment, and then, sadly) That's probably true.

(Doña Estrelita enters carrying a small jeweled casket.)

DR. BROWNE

And what about you? What do you want?

DOÑA ESTRELITA

The English are supposed to be gracious.

DR. BROWNE

You're an unexpected participant in these funeral games.

DOÑA ESTRELITA

I bring you trinkets, little toys.

DR. BROWNE

Trinkets.
You know me so well. Let me see.

DOÑA ESTRELITA

(Opening the casket, laying these things one by one in his lap) Torn scarlet lace.
A rosary.
A dry bit of blackroot.

DR. BROWNE

Explain these gifts.

DOÑA ESTRELITA

The scarlet lace. I wore it when I was young, attendant on my husband in the court of King James. The night I saw you for the first time. My weakness for men of learning.

DR. BROWNE

The winds that night. Drunkenness. They could barely keep the torches lit, the shutters banged like gunshot, the whole palace groaned.

DOÑA ESTRELITA

The rosary. I prayed for you till the silver beads tarnished black. And after you betrayed me, and fled from the scandal, I prayed for death.

DR. BROWNE

I prayed too.

DOÑA ESTRELITA

Faint heart, you never had the nerve.
The blackroot.

DR. BROWNE

Poison.

DOÑA ESTRELITA

Because prayers for death were insufficient . . .
I would have died for you. I bit my hands till they bled. I could have done it but . . . I survived and went home to Spain. And I have waited ever since . . .

DR. BROWNE

For what? Not for me, the wait's not worth it.

DOÑA ESTRELITA

To wait . . . for hatred to turn to love again.

DR. BROWNE

I thought you'd come on a timber ship. To take me home.

(Pause.)

DOÑA ESTRELITA

I have.

(She goes.
Browne watches her go. His Soul sits up and watches her leave as well. Maccabbee enters, carrying a large goblet of bubbling poison.)

MACCABBEE

You bin live and awake?
Dis is . . . sumpin da doctah wannetya ta drink. He . . . uh, he said it bin fer yer cough.

DR. BROWNE

(Facing away from him, deeply sad) I haven't got a cough.

MACCABBEE

Well, a ounce a prevention . . .

DR. BROWNE

Damn the doctor and his noxious drugs. Set it down somewhere.

MACCABBEE

Ah, come on, Doctah, open yer mouf 'n' I'll pour it in.

DR. BROWNE

(Turning suddenly on Maccabbee) I SAID SET IT DOWN, YOU NO-NOSE INSUBORDINATE, AND LEAVE ME BE.

(His rage causes another extremely painful intestinal explosion and tearing; Browne screams and clutches his side, holding tight to Estrelita's little trinket casket.)

DR. BROWNE

I want peace. All I want is p . . .

(Schadenfreude and Dogwater burst into the room, each with a huge manuscript.)

DR. DOGWATER

(Placing his manuscript on Browne's chest) A preliminary duh-draft of my eulogy.

DR. SCHADENFREUDE

(Following suit) And mine.

DR. DOGWATER

Chuh-choose. Muh-my speech affirms the justice of God, the rewards of a luh-life of industry, and your impressive eagerness to enter into Puh-Puh-Paradise.

DR. SCHADENFREUDE

Mine's a tastefully humorous recounting of the pathogenesis of your tumor.

DR. BROWNE

(Looking at the manuscripts) Such massive tomes. How can there possibly be so much to say about death?

DR. SCHADENFREUDE

I confess. I've been working on mine for a month.

DR. BROWNE

A month! I've only been ill three weeks!

DR. SCHADENFREUDE

Call it a hunch . . .

DR. DOGWATER

Now about the state or your, uh, estate . . .

DR. BROWNE

Never fear. Babbo has the Will in safekeeping and will read it to the assembled bereaved after my . . .

(Babbo enters.)

BABBO

Secuse me, Dr. Browne, but . . .

DR. DOGWATER

Y-you have entrusted your Wuh-Will to your cuh-cuh-cuh-*cook*?

DR. BROWNE

A trusted family servant. She nursed me when I was a baby. She nursed my father when he was a baby.

BABBO

I nurset yer grandfather too, but he han't bin no babbie, just lonely. He bin da most entertaining of da three.

DR. DOGWATER

Buh-buh-buh—

DR. BROWNE

Remain calm in the face of adversity, Dogwater. Take your example from me. Maccabbee, show the gentlemen out. Oh, and Schadenfreude. I'm not drinking that potion.

DR. SCHADENFREUDE

What potion? I sent no potion.

DR. BROWNE

Maccabbee said . . .

MACCABBEE

Uh, no, I said da doctah sent it, but I han't say which one.

DR. DOGWATER

Well I certainly didn't send it.

DR. SCHADENFREUDE

Nor I.

MACCABBEE

Right. It bin da other doctah.

DR. BROWNE

Another? Good God, there's *another* doctor in this house?

MACCABBEE

A verra famous specialist. He couldn't stay but he droppet da poison . . . I mean da potion off. Secuse me, Doctah. Dis way, Doctah. Doctah.

(They file out.)

DR. BROWNE

Babbo, what is that succulent aroma?

BABBO

Da chickens bin broasting like da souls a da damned.

(His Soul sinks again from view.)

DR. BROWNE

Here, consign these to the flames as well. Kindling.

(He hands Babbo the eulogies. Dorothy enters.)

DAME DOROTHY

Babbo, I apologize for . . .

BABBO

Da missus pinchet my tart. *(She exits)*

(Pause.)

DR. BROWNE

No more guests? No more people come to pay their respects, or demand payment, or . . .

DAME DOROTHY

Only me.

DR. BROWNE

I want to be forgiven all my sins, wife. It's very painful, burning.

DAME DOROTHY

There's no burning after, I think it's . . . a metaphor for something. You look dreadful.

DR. BROWNE

I am exceedingly taxed. I am completely terrified, you see.

DAME DOROTHY

I know.
I want to say good-bye, Thomas.

DR. BROWNE

No. Not you. No.

DAME DOROTHY

I'll wait with you.

DR. BROWNE

For what?

DAME DOROTHY

I don't know, I . . .

DR. BROWNE

For . . . Death.

I once sat down to write a meditation on Immortality. On the world free of death. Now there's a thought. *Hydriotaphia.* It's my best piece, it's very good, I recommend it. It was at the hanging I first knew, really knew, the possibility of my own death. It was at that trial, when those women were hanged, when they . . . when it was *my words* that hanged them, I . . . first knew, then, that I would die, and . . .
Their faces were mottled purple, like plums, waxy. The wood creaked under the weight of their bodies.
And I hoped to build with golden words a ladder up to Heaven, and in my final hour I'd remember what I'd written, and ascend.
(He is getting weaker)
Oh God I am talking myself to death.
Where is my soul? Escaped?
All my life . . . my words sought paths unknown to me. Along hidden tributaries they flowed and reached . . . unforseen conclusions. The battering complicatedness of living, it's . . . And there was no turning back. The light is always dying.
A fire, wife, I can't see you . . .

DAME DOROTHY
Here I am, Thomas. You look very far away.

DR. BROWNE
Dorothy, good-bye. The ship embarks at first wind. The mast and sails are gilded with blood, on seas of blood we sail, in search of prey. The nets hauled in by mighty hands, up from the red depths to the surface, up come the great black nets, full and heavy with the world's riches, hauled to the stronghold, to the drybone bank of death, with a hiss and suck plucked from the waters, in a ruby mist, in a fine red rain.
You . . . who must live through this . . . I pity you . . .

DAME DOROTHY
Thomas? THOMAS! Oh God, DOCTOR, DOCTOR!

(She runs out. His Soul sits up dazedly. Death enters, carrying his knife.)

DEATH

I've delayed too long; I must accomplish it. I weep for you, Thomas, this will hurt.

DR. BROWNE

Stay away from me, I won't have you touch me, I'm afraid of you, your knife . . .

DEATH

I need no tools. *(He drops the knife)* I have my hands. There is no mystery to this. It's ugly. A simple murder . . .

DR. BROWNE

I gave you my hand once, I was a child, how was I to know what you had in mind, that you'd leave me behind, alone in the forest, not deliver me out of the house of bondage but abandon me here to live in the valley of bones—traitor! Traitor! You never intended to save your boy!

(Death places his hands around Browne's neck.)

DEATH

Let me show you how I love you, child.
Words sometimes are not enough. My hands are more expressive.

DR. BROWNE

The hands of the silk merchant were delicate hands, used to spooling fine silk thread and not snapping it. I remember a soft caress, once, oh please, PLEASE, release me . . . *I can't move . . .*

DEATH

No.

Listen.
The machines in the quarry. Digging deep.
Boom. Booom. Booom. Boooom.

(With each "boom" Death tightens his grip on Dr. Browne's throat. Browne struggles wildly, horrible sounds, and then falls limp. It is violent and ugly. Finally, Dr. Browne is dead.
Death sighs, picks up the knife, looks at the body. He pries open Browne's mouth. Removing the Will from his coat pocket, Death folds it into a small square, places it inside Browne's mouth, and then gently pushes his mouth closed.)

DEATH

Thy Will be done.

(Death leaves.)

HIS SOUL

Good-bye.

(Maccabbee rushes in.)

MACCABBEE

Doctah? Doctah? WAKET UP!
Ah Christ . . . He . . . he bin dead fer real! *(Furious)* He died before I bin able ta kill him!

(His Soul wanders out from behind the bed, almost drunkenly, happy.)

HIS SOUL

(Looking down, dazed) Look. I've got *LEGS.*

MACCABBEE

I tried!

HIS SOUL

(Looking curiously about the room) Yeah, yeah . . .

MACCABBEE

I tried my best!

(His Soul sees the goblet of poison.)

HIS SOUL

I need a drink!

(It goes toward the goblet.)

MACCABBEE

Dat bin a mistaket.

HIS SOUL

(Picking up the goblet) Shut up.
(His Soul drinks) Mmmmm.

MACCABBEE

I tried! You saw!

HIS SOUL

Look! Legs!

(It exits toward the kitchen.)

MACCABBEE

BROWNE! YOU DIED TOO SOON! COME BACK! COME BACK!
(He sinks to his knees at the foot of Browne's bed. Brokenly) MY NOSE! MY NOSE!

Act Five

POST MORTEM

Black Night, Candlelight

The bed is stripped, covered in black, the room draped in mourning crepe. His Soul is sitting in a corner of the room, next to a pile of soiled bed linens. It is happily watching, smoking a cigarette and sipping from the goblet of poison.
Seated on the bed, Babbo is at work, sewing up the body of Browne in the shroud.

BABBO

(Singing:)
Dat old monstrah's come 'n' gone
'N' da babbie sleepet.
Dat old monstrah's come 'n' gone
'N' da babbie sleepet.
Dat old monstrah's took his fill;
'N' da babbie sleepet still

Nevah more ta waket.
Nevah more ta waket.

(She puts coins on his eyes, gathers up the shroud and, as she finishes the stitching, she tells a story, a bedtime story for a young child.)

BABBO

Oncet upon a time, dere bin an old woman, poor 'n' tired a life, 'n' God curset her wif a babbie though she han't food ta feed herself. 'N' she hiket down to da road, where da poor people trampet, 'n' sits bya side a da road 'n' say:
"Da first one passes by here bin dis kid's godfather, 'n' I han't caret who it bin."
'N' God come strollet by 'n' say, "I wanna be da godfather." But she rejeck God, causet she bin harful mad at him fer cursing her wif da kid inna first place.
'N' den da Devil come by 'n' express simila sentiments, offrin ta be da kid's godfather. But she rejeck da Devil too causet he han't nuffin ta offret except trouble, so she rejeck him.
'N' finally Death come walket by, 'n' he looket like a nightmare, 'n' da sun go blacket where he walk, but da woman light up 'n' say: "You bin da only true friend a mine, you da one thing I can hope fer 'n' know I han't be disappointet inna end."
So Death become da godfather a her kid, 'n' he christen him . . . Thomas. 'N' da kid growet up ta be a famous doctah wif da power a life 'n' death, 'n' den . . .
'N' den he died, a course.

(She's finished. She bites off the thread and leaves.
Schadenfreude and Doña Estrelita enter stealthily. They pull the body of Pumpkin's rummy out from under the bed. They place it next to Browne's corpse on the bed. Then they position themselves to lift Browne off the bed.)

DR. SCHADENFREUDE

Eins, zwei, drei . . .

(They lift and almost drop him, staggered by the weight.)

DR. SCHADENFREUDE

He weighs more than I'd expect.

DOÑA ESTRELITA

He seems to have gotten heavier . . . Sssssh! Someone's coming!

(They begin running with the body in one direction; Estrelita stops when she realizes they won't make it out of the room in time. Panicking, they toss Browne's body back on the bed, where it lands topsy-turvy atop the rummy's body. Schadenfreude and Estrelita hide. Babbo enters. Babbo sees the corpses all a-jumble.)

BABBO

Dat's funny.
Musta slippet.

(She straightens the bodies out, in the process reversing Browne and the rummy's bodies.)

BABBO

Nicet 'n' neat, dat bin more liket.
(Sniffs) Hooh! Sumpin stinket harful a cheap hooch, hope it han't bin me . . .

(Babbo starts to leave, then stops, thinks for a moment, turns back to the bed, counts the corpses silently: "One, two." Thinks a moment more, then runs out screaming.
Schadenfreude and Estrelita emerge from their hiding places and start to lift the wrong corpse.)

DR. SCHADENFREUDE

Do you think he'll fit?

DOÑA ESTRELITA

It's a very large oven. Everything reeks dreadfully of rum.

DR. SCHADENFREUDE

(Indicating the corpse still on the bed) Our dead ringer must have been a drinker; fortunately Thomas was fastidiously abstemious. It would be infelicitous to introduce a body supersaturated with highly flammable spirits to a roaring oven fire. There could be . . . an explosion!

DOÑA ESTRELITA

Hurry! No time to think!

(They exit, carrying the rummy's body. Dogwater enters.)

DR. DOGWATER

There but for the grace of God go I. We read of well-orchestrated d . . . d . . . final days. Like tuh-tightly written dramas. *This* . . . was not well made.

(The Abbess enters, crosses herself. She sees Dogwater and crosses herself again, more ostentatiously.)

THE ABBESS OF X

The Will?

DR. DOGWATER

The uh-ancient cuh-cook has it.

THE ABBESS OF X

Babbo? He gave it to Babbo?

DR. DOGWATER

Your brother may have lived a genius but he died a loo-lunatic.

(The Abbess leaves.)

DR. DOGWATER

Rah-runs in the family.

(Pumpkin enters.)

PUMPKIN

Pardon me, Pastah.

DR. DOGWATER

Cuh-come for him already? We hah-haven't performed the exequies yet.

PUMPKIN

Funeral bin tomorrow. I wannet ta talk to you, Pastah.

DR. DOGWATER

Not now, Pah-Pumpkin, I'm too dah-dah-distracted.

PUMPKIN

Bin a matter of business.

DR. DOGWATER

I'm listening.

PUMPKIN

I got summat you bin verra interstet ta learn, but I han't gonna tell ya fer free.

DR. DOGWATER

What could you possibly know that I—

PUMPKIN

It concernet da quarry. 'N' da Will.

(Little pause.)

DR. DOGWATER

What will it cuh-cost me, this information?

PUMPKIN

Ten shares a da quarry.

DR. DOGWATER

Tuh-ten . . . you must be juh-joking.

PUMPKIN

Small comparet to what it cost you not ta know what I knowet.

DR. DOGWATER

Well, nuh-naturally you'd say that but—

THE ABBESS OF X

(Emerging from the shadows) Pay it Leviticus.

DR. DOGWATER

Uh-eavesdropping?

THE ABBESS OF X

Of course. Does this information concern Dame Dorothy?

PUMPKIN

How you know dat?

DR. DOGWATER

Whuh-what could he possibly know about Duh-Dame D . . .

THE ABBESS OF X

He's her lover.

PUMPKIN

That han't so!

DR. DOGWATER

(Overlapping Pumpkin) Luh-luh-luh . . . Uh-*what*?

THE ABBESS OF X

I'm trained to track the scent of carnal sin. You're her lover. Now you have something we want—

DR. DOGWATER

Wuh-we?

THE ABBESS OF X

I spoke with Thomas before he died. I'm certain to be named in the Will. Partners. Gloria in Excelsis Deo.
As I was saying. *(To Pumpkin)* You know something we want, and we know something you want kept a secret. So we compromise. Three shares.

PUMPKIN

I han't care ef it bin a secret. 'Tis her worry. Ten shares.

THE ABBESS OF X

Dogwater, what's the local penalty for adultery?

DR. DOGWATER

Fuh-fuh-flogging. And thirty days in the stocks for fuh-fuh-fornicating.

PUMPKIN

Seven shares.

THE ABBESS OF X

Five.

PUMPKIN

Done
(Produces a document) Sign dis.

(Dogwater takes the document, reads it, looks at Pumpkin.)

DR. DOGWATER

Uh-it's already made out for fuh-five shares.

PUMPKIN

(Producing a pencil) I bin preparet ta compromise. Sign 'n' I talk.

(Dogwater signs. Pumpkin takes the document.)

PUMPKIN

As a fellow shareholder in da Walsingham Quarry I feel it bin my duty ta inform ya dat Dame Dorothy, da soon-ta-be majority shareholder, plans ta—

(Dorothy enters.)

DAME DOROTHY

Plans to what, Mr. Pumpkin?
Plans to do what?

(Dorothy and Pumpkin look at one another.)

PUMPKIN

I bin sorry, Dorfy, but you han't listet ta me.

(He shows her the document.)

PUMPKIN

It han't da hentire works, but it bin five shares, 'n' dat's better 'n' nuffin.

DAME DOROTHY

"Nuffin" is precisely what it is.
This man knows nothing of my affairs. He's swindled you.
How could he know my plans?

DR. DOGWATER

He . . . he—

THE ABBESS OF X

. . . is your lover.

DAME DOROTHY

Him! He's a commoner!
Hello Alice, I'd heard you'd returned from the dead.

PUMPKIN

I lovet you, Dorfy, but love han't lastet onna small holding farm.

DAME DOROTHY

A commoner and deluded.

THE ABBESS OF X

At the risk of being . . . indelicate. This afternoon around six I took a little stroll in the woods, Dorothy. There's a lovely clearing with beds of wildflowers.

DAME DOROTHY

Ah.

THE ABBESS OF X

Need I say which two people in this room were making use of those beds? He may not be your lover, Dorothy, but he must be a *very* close friend.

DAME DOROTHY

(To Pumpkin) Tell them. I interrupted you.

PUMPKIN

You tell.

DAME DOROTHY

With pleasure.
I plan to close the quarry and give the fields away, back to the people who—

DR. DOGWATER

DUH-DO WHAT? YOU PLAN TO DO WHAT?

DAME DOROTHY

Walsingham Fields will be common lands again.

THE ABBESS OF X

Dorothy, that's insane.

DAME DOROTHY

Babbo told me about your visions, Alice. I'd be careful calling other people insane.

DR. DOGWATER

This is the fuh-final straw. You're mad, wuh-woman. The cuh-corporation will stop you, you'll be prevented—

THE ABBESS OF X

Sit, down, Leviticus, you're apoplectic.

(Schadenfreude enters.)

DR. SCHADENFREUDE

Ah, my dear Dogwater.

DR. DOGWATER

Whuh-where's that Wuh-Will! Where's that Guh-Goddamn cuh-cook?

DOÑA ESTRELITA

(Entering) Stay out of the kitchen! I just put a very large roast in the oven!

DR. SCHADENFREUDE

And look what I found in the oven fire!

(He displays a charred, smoking, thick manuscript) My eulogy! Yours, I regret to say, I was unable to save . . .

DR. DOGWATER

My eu-eu-eu-eu . . . *(He runs out)*

DR. SCHADENFREUDE

(As Dogwater flees) I tried my best to pluck it from the inferno, but your prose, alas, is infinitely drier than mine.

PUMPKIN

Dorfy, could we go—

DAME DOROTHY

Mrs. Browne, please. Your services won't be required till tomorrow morning. Not at all, in fact. I'll find someone more fit to bury my husband. He was right about you, you are too . . . tense.

PUMPKIN

As a shareholder I gotta right ta hear da Will readet.

DAME DOROTHY

Then sit in a corner somewhere and please refrain from speaking to me.

(The ranters enter.)

SARAH

We come ta see da houtcome.

RUTH

(Looking at the corpse) It look verra satisfactory.

(The rumble in the fields is heard, ominous.)

MARY

Da best bin yet ta comet.

DR. DOGWATER

(Reentering) Ranters, nuns and foreigners. This place is a fuh-frigging zuh-zoo.

MACCABBEE

(Entering) Da cook bin comet.
(He sees His Soul) Why hantchoo ascendet?

(His Soul takes a drag on the cigarette, looks at Maccabbee, looks up to Heaven.)

HIS SOUL

That is a very interesting question.
(Calling out to the audience) Is there a theologian in the house?
(It lifts the cup of poison, makes a toasting gesture, and drinks more poison) To your health, you snoutless procrastinator.

MACCABBEE

Han't rubbet in.

HIS SOUL

I'm *famished.* I gotta get a bite to eat. *(Exits)*

(Babbo enters; she's been drinking to fortify her nerves.)

DR. DOGWATER

Well hah-hallelujah! It's the kuh-kuh-queen of Heaven!

BABBO

Thank Gawd, dere bin da correck numba a cadavahs. Musta been delucinatet.

DAME DOROTHY

I think we ought to sing a hymn. In the memory of.

DR. SCHADENFREUDE

Hear hear! May I suggest "Oh Mein Gott, Du Rhüst So Denken Geschmecktet Dört die Himmelplatz Abfärht"?

DR. DOGWATER

Ah, pluh-please! We'll suh-sing an English hymn. *(To Schadenfreude) Barbarian.* "There Is a Land of Pure Delight."

BABBO

Oh, dat bin one a my favorites.

DR. DOGWATER

Well, anything to puh-please you, Your Guh-Grace.
In Memory: Sir Thomas Browne.

THE ABBESS OF X

Requiescat in Pace.

EVERYONE

(Sings:)
There is a land of pure delight
Where saints immortal reign.
Infinite day excludes the night
And pleasure banish pain.
There everlasting spring abides,
And never-withering flowers.
Death like a narrow sea divides
This heavenly land from ours.
Amen.

DR. DOGWATER

Nuh-now the Will.

THE ABBESS OF X

Read it, Babbo. You have the Will? . . .

BABBO

Well, I misplacet it, but . . .

(Dogwater lunges for the Bible.)

DR. DOGWATER

But here it is!

(He opens the Bible, and pulls out long shreds of paper.)

DR. DOGWATER

Wuh-what the fuh-fuh-fuh-

(The Abbess meanwhile has lunged at the mattress and retrieved the Will hidden there.)

THE ABBESS OF X

Forget it, Leviticus, the Will of Browne is here!

(She tears open the seal, as Dogwater lunges for the document. There is a brief snarling tug-of-war; the Abbess wins, doubling Dogwater over with a well-placed kick.)

THE ABBESS OF X

I begin to suspect you *enjoy* this trouncing, Leviticus.

DR. DOGWATER

(Clutching his privates) I cuh-could get used to it.

THE ABBESS OF X

(Speed reading through the Will) AHA! Here! "And all my shares in the Walsingham Quarry I bequeath to my dearly beloved wife Dorothy B—"

(She instantly starts to rip the Will into shreds. Dorothy rushes to stop her.)

DAME DOROTHY

What are you . . . IT TOOK ME TWO-AND-A-HALF HOURS TO WRITE THAT—Oops.

THE ABBESS OF X

(Rushing to the bed) IT'S A FAKE! WE'LL SEARCH FOR THE—

DAME DOROTHY

If you're looking for *your* version, Alice, here it is.

(Dorothy hurls a cloud of black ash in the Abbess's face.)

THE ABBESS OF X

You . . . You *burned* it!?!

(The Abbess lunges at Dorothy, Pumpkin intercedes, the Abbess flips him head over heels.)

DAME DOROTHY

Thank you, Alice, you must teach me how that's done.

DR. SCHADENFREUDE

Through the Will the dead speak to the living, and Browne remains for once uncharacteristically mum. Through the eulogy the living speak to the dead, and since I am the only one prepared to eulogize the deceased when the king arrives—

DR. DOGWATER

UH-I am prepared!

DR. SCHADENFREUDE

Your eulogy, Doctor, is toast.

DR. DOGWATER

(Triumphantly!) I have cuh-cuh-committed it to muh-memory!

(They square off, preparing to duel. Dogwater begins, in a singsongy ecclesiastical tenor:)

DR. DOGWATER

"Our Huh-Holy Fuh-Father, who does not suh-suffer us that we should know the hour of our d-departing, nuh-no more that we shuh-should know the duh-destination of our suh-soul on its puh-perilous fuh-final fuh-flight . . ."

DR. SCHADENFREUDE

(Reading, fast aggressive and loud) "Honored, esteemed friends and neighbors and fellow citizens of Norfolk, and most especially Your Majesty, before the full auric effulgency and pearline dazzlements of whose presence I am nearly but fortunately not entirely overwhelmed and at a loss of words, confronted with whose Jovian and may I be forgiven for saying it remarkably pleasing and attractive countenance the mere sight of which . . ."

(They are getting louder and louder, trying to outshout one another.)

DR. DOGWATER

(Continues his speech from above) ". . . compared to huh-whose stark and tuh-terrible Ma-ajesty we are as guh-giddy as mayflies, luh-loathsome as eels, wicked and heedless and damnable as vuh-vixen and vultures, lowly and vuh-vomitous as the cah-carrion of the earth; God Almighty in Huh-His infinite muh-mercy has taken fuh-from us our duh-dear Sir Thomas Buh-Browne, and in his puh-parting we should rejoice and make muh-merry, we should cuh-clap our hands and suh-sing hymns of laudation and thuh-thanksgiving, we shuh-should eat ruh-robustly and—"

DR. SCHADENFREUDE

(Continues his speech from above) ". . . inspires, conjures, calls forth in me, an inexpressibly grateful recipient for lo these many years of this most exceedingly delightful serene and salubrious island's world-renowned grace and hospitality, the ten-

derest and yet most thrillingly exalted of memories and recollections of my many many many many years of exquisitely intimate acquaintance with our Sir Thomas Browne, whom I was pleased to call friend, patient, *confidante*, now departed, gone gone gone gone, and yet, with all these memories, we haven't lost him—No! Allow me to share a few dozen of the most select with you. Ah I remember the day we met, it was—"

(The dueling eulogists are toe to toe, shrieking with rage at one another, ready to come to blows, when Babbo blows a shrill whistle. They stop, everyone turns to her.)

BABBO

I got da Will.
It bin in da tart. Den da tart disappearet. Den I findet da tart, but da Will han't bin in it. Den I foundet da Will, and I put it back inna tart. And den da missus took it from me, da Will *and* da tart. And den I foundet da Will. *(Little maddening pause)* Not da tart. Just da Will. One lastet time—

DAME DOROTHY

Found it? Where?

BABBO

(Almost a whisper) In da doctah's mouth. Aftah he bin dead.

DR. DOGWATER

Thuh-then huh-whose . . . ?

THE ABBESS OF X

(Over Dogwater's line above) Whose Will is it?

(From the urn, a great blast of smoke belches forth!
Everyone screams in terror and falls to the floor as, in the doorway leading to the kitchen, Dr. Browne is standing. He is slim, dressed in dark splendid Restoration clothing, which though not mouldering

and decayed, look a bit like Death's costume. Browne is pale but quite elegant.)

DR. BROWNE

This is the Last Will and Testament of Sir Thomas Browne, Doctor of Norfolk, Author.
(He enters the room)
My will is . . . to eat. To greedily engorge without restraint and know not eating death. I wake up, I wake up moments after dying—hungry. My life I spent defeating my hunger, I conquered my hunger by eating the world, and yet my hunger will live, it will live on after me, I will *be* hunger. Every gift I ever gave I want to retrieve; every cent I ever paid in tax or wage or purchase I want to steal back; every morsel in the mouth of every child ever fed by food procured with the money I spent I long to snatch back and eat and surfeit and die and disassemble and dust and disappear . . .
(He considers his corpse on the bed for an instant, and then) And most of all my name, I want to devour! And most of all, all the words, the words words words! I want to eat my words! Come flooding back to me, my words, unmake the world, the world I made by writing, undo it all, my every word, flood back into my blistered broken mouth and stop it up like clay, forever!
(Pause)
And for all the piddling rest of it, the house, the gold, the quarry . . . Well of course Dorothy I leave it all to you. To whom else, wife? Companion of my life. I leave everything to you.
(To the rest of them) So much fuss and bother . . . I suppose it gave the supporting cast something to do. While waiting for the end.

(The rumble from the fields again.)

DR. BROWNE

The end has come.

And tell the children, tell my friends, my foes, the future—
NO. Don't tell them ANYTHING.

(The notes of the Dies Irae *sound, faintly. From the kitchen, a warm red glow, drifts of smoke.*
Sarah sniffs. Browne, looking at her briefly, also sniffs. Then he sniffs again.)

DR. BROWNE

I wonder . . . what's cooking . . . in the kitchen?

(He exits through the door from which he entered. Before he disappears from view, he raises his arms. Immediately, a big fiery explosion from the kitchen. A hot red glow in the windows. A very serious fire.)

DAME DOROTHY

A fire, fire in the kitchen!

(She runs out. Schadenfreude and Doña Estrelita look at each other.)

DOÑA ESTRELITA

Perhaps we put the wrong corpse in the oven.

DR. SCHADENFREUDE

Uh oh!

(Schadenfreude and Doña Estrelita run out.)

DR. DOGWATER

(Looking out the window) Oh duh-dear, the thatch is catching. The whole west wing is gah-going up.

THE ABBESS OF X

What's that noise?

(The rumbling again, very deep, very low, very loud, and the sounds of mighty whirling winds, and a far-off sound of shouts and screams.)

DR. DOGWATER

The ruh-roof caving in, puh-probably.

THE ABBESS OF X

No, another noise, from outside . . .

(The sounds outside increase, the room grows darker.)

RUTH

Mary, what be dat soundet?

MARY

Soundet like it come from da general direction a da quarry.

DR. DOGWATER

The quarry?

(The sound suddenly gets much worse, a terrible, appalling, bone-rattling, theater-shaking, crashing, roaring, imploding sound—the worst sound ever heard, the sound of the world ending. Under it, or over it, the Dies Irae *again. The lights in the candles flicker out as the room grows terribly dark. In the windows a sick green light.)*

DR. DOGWATER

Oh my Guh-God!

(The Abbess, Pumpkin and Dogwater rush out. Ruth and Mary follow them. The terrible roaring and imploding continues, on and on. Bits of plaster fall from the ceiling. Babbo and Maccabbee cower together. Sarah stands, thrilled by the pandemonium, and bows. The sound begins to die, the lights restore.)

BABBO

Dis han't a atmospheret conducive ta grief.

(There is a moist explosion, like something big and wet popping.)

MACCABBEE

Wonder what dat be?

BABBO

It comet from da pantry.

MACCABBEE

Da chicken! Da chicken explodet!

(He runs off. His Soul enters from the kitchen, soot-blackened, smoking a cigarette, carrying a goblet.)

HIS SOUL

(Ear to the ground) I hear something. Underground. Tunneling, scurrying, it's . . . *Moles.*
I feel *awful.*

(Doña Estrelita enters, Schadenfreude close behind her. She flings herself on the body of Browne.)

DOÑA ESTRELITA

Thomas, good-bye, I have failed in my mission!

DR. SCHADENFREUDE

Doña!

DOÑA ESTRELITA

What?

DR. SCHADENFREUDE

I assume you have connections at court.

DOÑA ESTRELITA

When I am in London the queen and I visit cemeteries together. We make tombstone rubbings.

DR. SCHADENFREUDE

The office of king's physician.

DOÑA ESTRELITA

I know a brilliant Norfolk doctor of German extraction who simply *must* be appointed!

DR. SCHADENFREUDE

And you, great lady, will receive the ashes of your love, in a small box, by parcel post!

DOÑA ESTRELITA

But how—

DR. SCHADENFREUDE

They'll put him in the ground, I'll dig him up. Child's play! I too have an oven . . .

(She kisses him, a long hot kiss on the mouth.)

DOÑA ESTRELITA

I must go. My ship departs Brighton at sunrise.

(She starts out.)

DR. SCHADENFREUDE

Wait!
(He lifts the urn, hands it to her)
A souvenir . . .

(She accepts it and bows. They exit.
Dorothy enters, sooty and disheveled and numbed.)

DAME DOROTHY

Oh. Let it burn, there are far too many rooms in this house anyway. The west wing was where the children lived. It won't be missed.

(She sits on the bed next to Browne's body.
The Abbess enters in a big hurry. She says a very fast prayer over the corpse, and then heads out the door.)

BABBO

Where ya headet, Alice?

THE ABBESS OF X

It's a sign from God! Back to France! *(Exits)*

BABBO

(Calling after) Have a good swim, Alice.

(Dogwater, Pumpkin, Ruth and Mary enter from outside.)

DR. DOGWATER

Bah-bah-bah-

PUMPKIN

Da quarry, bin *gone*!

RUTH

Congratulations, Sarah, bin some curse.

PUMPKIN

Da machines . . . drillet, hit a giant cavern underneaf, 'n' . . . da ground split, 'n' da whole works just fall right in. Gone. From da rim you han't see da bottom. 'Tis a verra abyss.

SARAH

Gone ta hell.

(The ranters embrace one another.)

RUTH AND MARY

Yisroel 'n' Judah!

(The ranters rush outside again.)

DR. DOGWATER

The expense, the overhead, it's the end of the wuh-world.

PUMPKIN

'Tis unfair! My shares bin swallowet! I worket hard fer dem.

DAME DOROTHY

Poor Pumpkin, you always wind up with a pit, in a rut, with a hole in the ground. God beshrew my heart, but I pity you.

PUMPKIN

(Looking at her hard for a moment, then) You han't gotta do dat. Dis hurt me sumpin harful but I bin a descendant a a sturdy race. Fuck da countryside. I go to London.
(To Dorothy again, with cold hatred) I han't feel nuffin. *(He exits)*

DR. DOGWATER

Y-yes. Not to dah-despair. I've luh-lost everything. *(To Dorothy)* But then again so have *yuh-you.* Thuh-that's some cuh-comfort.
Guh-God moves in mah-mysterious and sometimes ruh-rather malicious ways. To spur us on. And we go on. We duh-dare not do otherwise.

(Dogwater exits as the ranters return.)

SARAH

Dorothy.

DAME DOROTHY

I can't rise, I've taken root.

SARAH

Listet, babbie. In ten days dere be a ship sailet from Portsmouth. 'N' me 'n' Mary 'n' Ruth be on It. It sail fer da new world.

MARY

Sail fer America.

RUTH

Dere bin endless land dere, belonget ta no one. Only savages.

MARY

We maket a community dere, a fellow creatures.

SARAH

Da new world, Dorothy. Bin you comet?

(Dorothy stands slowly.)

DAME DOROTHY

First I have to bury my husband.

SARAH

Portsmouth. Da ship bin callet *Circe.* Circe bin a Greek witch.

(The ranters go.)

HIS SOUL

(Sings:)
Happily I turn the earth,
tunneling for all I'm worth.
Who needs Heaven, who needs souls?
Below is Paradise for moles . . .

DAME DOROTHY

Good-bye, husband. We've populated the earth. We'll have our grandchildren, never fear, the children were only waiting for you to go. And generations will descend, down through the centuries, cursed by our gold, Browne upon Browne.
I'll go my solitary way to America, and maybe I'll marry again. I'll bring only one possession:
(She holds up a slender, elegant book, reads from the title page)
"Hydriotaphia or Urne-Buriall," by Sir Thomas Browne.
I'll read it to children to help them fall asleep at night. Your words. To turn into pure music in their heads as they dream.

(She kisses the corpse's forehead and leaves.)

HIS SOUL

(Sings:)
Heaven's bright and full of fluff,
And never is there dirt enough,
So Heaven's not where moles are found
But digging deeper
Deeper deeper
Always deeper underground . . .

(Speaking, looking over the audience, the room, the theater with great wonder and awe and joy) My *goodness.* So *this* is what the earth is like. So this is what a *body* is. So this is what people are. It's been *quite* an experience.
(Holding up goblet) And this concoction is delicious! And these *cigarettes,* well, *yum yum,* I recommend cigarettes to every —Um. Urk. *(A violent spasm of the gut)* Uh oh.
(Another spasm)
This is anticlimactic, don't you think? Oh, well.

(His Soul dies, collapsing in the pile of soiled laundry. A faint, distant, solemn single church bell chimes.)

MACCABBEE

(Entering) My nose! Lookit! Lookit at my nose! Tell me I han't been dreamet!

BABBO

It han't bronzet no more!

MACCABBEE

Resurrectet! A fleshly proboscis as in days a yore!

BABBO

Praise Gawd! It been a mackerel!

MACCABBEE

Verra! Chicken C! It burstet! 'N' inside dere bin maggots! 'N' da maggots sproutet wings, 'n' dey bin flies! 'N' da flies growet black 'n'gold, 'n' turnet inta bees! 'N' da bees maket honey, clover honey, 'n' honey cover da walls, run on da floor, sweet honey, smella clover, fields in flower, 'n' I accosted myself, "Maccabbee," I says, "draw a long deep breath a dis miracleous perfume!" 'N' I drawet, 'n' den . . . Outta dat dead metal comet dis livet protuberance! Alive, alive, 'tis verra nice indeed.

(He inhales. She inhales.)

BABBO

Dat laundry reeket. Tomorrow we burnet.

MACCABBEE

Dere bin good smells 'n' bad, 'n' eiver one gets me going.

(They look at each other.)

BABBO

You wanna?

MACCABBEE

(Looking at His Soul) Poor babbie.
Poor Dr. Browne. God bless his soul.

BABBO

Hamen.

MACCABBEE

I wanna.

BABBO

Mordal sin. It bin a long, long day.

(They come together as lights go to black and . . .)

DA VERRA END

An Afterword

WHEN *Hydriotaphia* was in preparation at Berkeley Rep, with rehearsal time severely limited, I wrote a series of sketchy suggestions for Jonathan Hadary to consider while constructing his Browne. Jonathan greeted the pages I'd prepared with a wonderfully weary and slightly incredulous smile, accepting them graciously, promising to read them; actors know how to handle a control freak. I knew better than to ever ask if he had read them. A magnificent actor, Jonathan made Browne entirely his own.

It's a tricky part, Dr. Browne is, and the entire extended farce relies very heavily, in terms of sustained tension and antic forward motion, on the performance of the title role. Publishing these notes is a risky and problematic decision. I don't mean to suggest that there is only one way the good Doctor can be played. But the notes might be a useful guide for an actor or director who is beginning to think about the part, and perhaps non-actors and non-directors will find them illuminating vis-à-vis the performance aspects of the text.

Some General Thoughts about Browne:

Stephen Spinella, for whom the part of Browne was written, watched Bette Davis movies in preparation; one great queen learning from another, the waspishness and the wit. He even modeled his hair and makeup ever so subtly after Bette's. For whatever it's worth . . .

Heinrich Heine, the great nineteenth century German-Jewish poet, in horrific pain for *eight years* in his bed in Paris, was apparently all through his ordeal a dazzling conversationalist whose voice betrayed nothing of his torment, and even though he almost never slept he wrote over a thousand magnificent poems from his bed.

Browne's a writer and he loves words.

He's very very very afraid of dying, and of Death.

Everything internal he shares with his audience.

When others are onstage, if he wants them to be in the room he greedily engages with them. Otherwise, he tries various stratagems to expel them. He almost never ignores anyone. All his life he has been observing and watching and thinking about what he watches and observes.

He's appalled by the way others treat him and the way they treat the fact of his incipient demise—from Babbo's discussion of the funeral food to Dogwater's carping about the Will, he is aghast. Their matter-of-fact acceptance, even in some cases their eagerness for his death, wounds and shocks him.

He has a good sense of humor.

His body has failed him but his mind is alert. There is rarely grogginess or weakness. His body is simply swollen, toxic, useless. The head is wide awake. What is killing him is his guts exploding.

He frequently turns on a dime, emotionally.

He never relaxes! He is active, his mind is working fast, even frantically, either to try to save himself, to distract himself from his terror and pain, or to meet his death head-on by shoving people away and facing being alone with his terror and pain.

None of these actions work—he is *always* returned to the fact he states at the top of the play: "I will die today."

Act One

Browne wakes up, immediately wide awake, into terror, knowing that something frightening (Death's first appearance) has just occurred.

He instantly calls for his comfort—Maccabbee—to ascertain if this morning is his birthday. It is—and he knows that he will die today.

The fear that realization engenders sets his busy mind to work. He wants to see the gravedigger—he wants to see the man who is fucking his wife.

The screaming at his wife makes his belly hurt, badly, for a moment. ("I shouldn't scream, it brings on the bloating.") Babbo's questions about the food pull him out of the pain, her fondness for him (". . . such a fussy 'n' patricula man.") calms him a little and he tells her about the dream he has had the previous night.

The dream is painted by him (the writer!) in quick sure simple strokes, a harsh little poem. I may be dying but I can still do this! And do it well!

This cheers him a little—enough to engage with her joke. ("There should be tears!")

The quarry engines call to him. He loves them; he loves what he owns, what he has made, his world ("*My* engines!")—and HE DOES NOT WANT TO DIE.

Schadenfreude comes in—Browne believes his leeches will help. The treatment almost kills him. He passes out.

While unconscious: he dreams that the gravedigger is screwing his wife. And then he dreams about moles. The moles are dark, beautiful, sexy and frightening. He dreams about the urn, also frightening, and inviting.

He wakes up: Dogwater's yelling blasts him wide awake, instantly out of sleep and scrambling to locate himself—"Am I dead?"—and when he realizes (instantly!) that he's still alive, he immediately assesses and deals with the menace of the moles; demanding of his wife that she fetch the gravedigger, he looks for the urn.

It annoys him that Dogwater is here, and that he's intruding, he knows what Dogwater wants. He decides to torture Dogwater a little, pretending not to know him (he pretends successfully, we don't need to know that it's pretending), putting him in his place with his credentials ("I studied in Padua . . ."), and as always with his ability to dazzle with words ("Unearth the urn . . .").

And as always the words take him to the truth—that he is going to die. And that he cannot face dying. ("It is impossible to CONCLUDE *anything*.")

He abandons the game with Dogwater. It offends him that Dogwater is demanding a look at his Will. They don't love him, the pastor only wants the money to be secured, and his wife is only interested in inheriting it and marrying the gravedigger. He decides to deny that he has written one. He wants to watch them writhe.

Having hooked them, he dismisses them.

He gives the Will to Babbo to hide, the only person he trusts.

His Soul, which has been noisily berating him more and more in the past week, demands that he let her go—that he die. He would like to believe that she is the best part of him and if he releases, if he dies, she will ascend and he will live in Eternity. But he is afraid to die, and like everyone else, she doesn't love him, she only wants something from him; he decides to refuse her as well. He listens for his quarry engines, their love song to him, and he lets them lull him to sleep, escaping her demand.

While unconscious: asleep, he dreams of a timber ship. Someone is on the ship, though he cannot see who it is. The ship frightens him. He squirms a bit in fear.

He wakes up: Ruth's "EARFEN CLOT" wakes him in two stages—eyes closed, he sits up, seeing the scary timber ship on the cold river.

His eyes pop open—he is wide awake. And alone. And scared. He calls for company—His Soul—let's argue some more! But it's gone. He is frightened by its disappearance. He tries to reassure himself by saying, as any rational person would, that it doesn't exist: "Losing you is less than losing nothing . . ." To distract himself from the fear, to be alone no longer, he calls for the comforting presence of a manservant.

Browne orders the chicken experiment.

This begins as a distraction but he as usual is led by his mind to a search for the truth—that he really wants to know whether the soul exists, whether it has substance, as His Soul now seems to have. He is used to using Maccabbee to think these things through; Maccabbee makes him explain and that helps clarify—he has always known himself to be too impulsive and quick.

But he hears himself distracting himself ("You're right. It is . . . nuts."), and remembers what is REALLY frightening here—dying. ("Why is there no one here to comfort me?") He is embarrassed that he's reduced to asking this clod for company, revealing so much of himself . . .

So Browne sends Macc away.

But he's lonely and frightened, he changes his mind, calls Maccabbee back. The moles, the menace, do something about it, kill the bastards. ("A mixture of cyanide and boiling lye . . .")

He hears himself again, and again angrily sends Maccabbee away, making sure as he leaves that he's going to do the experiment (This sort of moment is what Estrelita is referring to when she says, "You are split in two . . ."), because Browne really needs to know . . .

AND HERE—he has a spasm of pain. He feels things giving inside. He tries to metaphoricize it (to control it): "The ropes on the dock are slipping from the moorings, and I'm . . . off . . ." ANOTHER SPASM OF PAIN—and he's out.

A moment (Macc's little speech: "Fetch da rottet birds . . .") and he is suddenly jolted awake by a third SPASM which is so severe it knocks him out cold.

While unconscious (this corresponds to Death's and the Abbess's entrances toward the end of the Act): he dreams a terrible terrible dream. His dead father is in the room with a huge kitchen knife: when Browne was a child his father used it when drunk to menace his mother, and him.

He is so frightened by this vision that he decides to flee the room by letting His Soul go—by dying. ("Into your hands I . . . COMMEND MY . . .") And there it is, eagerly awaiting his demise, which pisses him off, and frightens him; he changes "commend" into "condemn" and decides to wake up instead, and when he does, to his horror, confronts his dead sister (GASP!) and dead father! (GASP!) This cannot be ("NO!").

And they go away.

He is now fully awake: Dorothy and Dogwater rush in. He asks if this can have been real. He's sure he saw them. The sight of his father is by leagues the most terrifying thing he's ever seen. In the midst of his terror, the ship returns as an image to him—but it's a different ship, another ship, not the coffin ship, but . . . some vessel bringing love. He looks for and finds his quarry engines' love song. Again, he lets them lull him to sleep, leaving a last little poem in the air, a talisman to protect him while he sleeps, protect him from terrible Father Dead.

While unconscious: he sleeps, dreaming of the ship, solace, protection.

Act Two

Browne begins to wake at Babbo's, "DON'T DIE, DOCTAH . . ."

He has been dreaming of rescue, love, warmth on the timber ship. He feels happy calm and peaceful. Someone who loves him has come for him. He has been very cold and he asks for warmth, which he gets from her.

Then she leaves. ("The sun . . .") He is cold again. He opens his eyes (". . . clouds over . . .").

And he wakes up into a nightmare—terrible Father Dead is back. He hides under the covers, completely abjectly terror-stricken.

It works! He is still terrified ("I cannot see that face again."), but there was comfort for him in the room just a moment ago—a Spanish Lady . . . ?

His Soul is back, furious as ever; but Browne has just triumphed over Death (by hiding from him) and is determined to triumph over it too, denying its existence ("You're not my soul, either, just some malcontented noisy thing . . ."), straining to shit out the tumor, and when he can't do that—telling her that everything he has is his and his alone—he will not comply with its request—he won't give up anything ("It's all mine . . ."). Everything has been created by his desire and his intellect and none of it belongs to anyone else.

His Soul reminds him that the writing was a collaboration. He has considerable pride in what he has accomplished ("I recorded it for posterity!"), but His Soul reminds him how immensely beautiful and clean and pure and holy its song was, and he knows that what he wrote was none of those things: his words took him to places he didn't anticipate, to a darkness and meaninglessness at the center of existence, to a void.

That's what is in the three ellipses, in Act One ("The baby in the . . . the genesis of things."), here in Act Two ("When I described what I saw inside, the room had changed, it . . . was rather empty, and") and in Act Four ("The battering complicatedness of living, it's . . ."), it's a very human place, where opposites coexist and overwhelm and intoxicate and affright—and for which no words exist—which is why this place, this ellipsis, draws him in and frightens him so . . . Browne can describe everything but he cannot describe that. It is a dark and bitter realization, a dark and bitter place, and the fact that he is actually rather fascinated by it makes it only worse, he feels ashamed, alarmed . . .

Browne feels he should be pitied rather than despised for this. ("Pity me! You should! The world made me, the word betrayed me, I never wanted to see . . .")

So that when Maccabbee comes back in, Browne is in a very troubled place; he feels that he has failed God, who sent him this beautiful song, which he then smudged and besmirched, simply by being flawed, greedy, fearful—human.

He doesn't want to deal with Maccabbee. At first he has no idea what Macc's talking about, strangling chickens—and when he remembers the experiment it seems like a pathetic joke, incredibly ridiculous considering what he's just realized, his failure, his shame. He wants this torment to end (". . . let's end this farce . . .").

But as always when he arrives at Death's doorstep, ready to face it, he finds he can't. ("What were the results?")

And Browne is alarmed to hear that the results are something unexpected—the unknown, the weirdness, that really scares him, really makes mock of his attempts to control this day. WHAT IS GOING ON HERE!? ("IT CANNOT CONCEIVABLY WEIGH *MORE* DEAD THAN . . .")

This connects to what he says in Act Four, and it's at the heart of the terror—("It isn't possible! I can't conceive it!")—that there is something in this dying business that he with all his intellect cannot control.

And then just as he is getting really frantic and scared, this death portent, the Weaver of Shrouds, appears, and in trying to get away from her, and this terrible fear, and this room, to physically get away, he causes something in his swollen gut to rip. He tries to deal with this physical crisis, and with the frightening weaver, and in the midst of all this Father Dead appears, and Browne curls away from him into a little ball at the uppermost corner of the bed—hiding worked once before, and he has to calm this fire in his gut—and calls/begs for the psalm. The psalm reassures him, he takes a peek and sees Death has gone . . .

The doctor arrives, unfortunately the wrong one.

During the prayers he takes inventory of his innards: he realizes that he has done some serious damage to himself and that as he said at the beginning of the day, he is, in fact, going to die, and soon. He is as he says "working on it."

Dogwater comes at Browne demanding the Will. Browne doesn't want to give it to him, he is frightened, he wants to live, he tries to get some distraction action going by talking about/railing against his children, attacking Dorothy, keeping Dogwater at bay—he makes a last stab at hanging on, roaring.

But as always his words lead him back to death, bitterness, regret. ("He used to send copies to me, but then he . . . stopped.") Dorothy's, "You got what you wanted," is painful to hear. He is returned to the bad place—while the doctors fight and Dogwater storms off—and perhaps even Dogwater's, "This is what comes of you irresponsibility," gets to Browne. He makes a decision, the net result of all that has happened so far: he decides he is ready to end it.

This is a big change: though there will be moments when he thinks otherwise, from this point on for the rest of the play Browne is trying to face dying, he is trying to die.

He asks to go to the river, which he knows will finish him off—he makes the request first of Schadenfreude, then of Dorothy. Browne tries to get out of bed on his own power; unable to do that, he asks the weaver.

Even though this is his last request, as he says, even though he has resolved to go, no one will help.

Then help arrives. The woman from the ship. It is astonishing, a miracle, an unexpected occurrence that is for a change favorable, reassuring.

While she talks to Schadenfreude, Browne watches her closely and realizes who she is. It's a private realization, the audience doesn't need to see it, but probably it comes here. By the time Browne asks her, "How did I know you were coming to me?" he knows who she is.

When he says, "How mysterious," he is referring to her astonishing arrival at just this juncture. There is real grief and regret in, "I think now I never thought enough about love." Here is a mystery Browne didn't plumb deeply enough, and now it's really too late.

And then he goes off to the river.

At the River: the washing is extremely lovely, though he is unconscious for most of it.

Act Three

Asleep while being bathed, dried, carried back from the river to the house: in his dream the moles have changed into something quite sexy and wonderful, full of mystery and delight.

He half-wakes: Dogwater's yelling brings him up to the surface waking, and he tries to describe vast twisty enticing tunnels under the river, full of moles—and even half-awake Browne composes poems, this one about moles, their blindness seeming deep and full of powerful meaning—blind perhaps like a seer, or a prophet, tragic and yet deep diggers, like Browne himself, nosing through the earth for the truth.

There is groggy joy in making the poem.

Act Four

During the Rant: the lovely warmth and ease and caress of the bath is banished in the rant. All the things Browne regrets and is ashamed of, all his terror of dying is called forth in this nightmare, ending with a premonition of the hunger that comes after—this is when, during the rant, he cries.

He wakes up: Dorothy's, "BABBO!" wakes him, and again he wakes into terror, alone.

After he tries to shit, he has a spasm—what ripped intestinely in Act Two is worsening. Browne realizes that he is in trouble, nearing the end.

The urn has arrived, a death portent, silent, still . . .

He is terrified still of dying, he remembers the Capuchin Catacombs in Rome, how sad and disappointed those faces were, how horrible . . .

Maccabbee enters. Browne sends him to get the gravedigger—unfinished business. Babbo arrives to tell him Alice is here. ("She wannet me ta prepare ya fer da shock.") He is very much afraid to see her, he calls Maccabbee back to delay that moment, and also to tell him what it looks like, inside that urn . . .

It's as bad as Browne thought. All delays lead him back to the fear. Maccabbee's no use—and here Browne decides to face these terrible tasks, Alice, the gravedigger, dying . . . Browne sends Maccabbee away.

He tries to prepare for the shock of seeing Alice, asking Babbo what she's like. Babbo goes to fetch her, leaving Browne alone for a moment with the urn.

He tries to control the fear of it, of that stillmouth, by making a little epigram, a little poem line, an apostrophe. ("Oh open urn . . .")

An unexpected and scary surprise. The spume of dust. Browne freaks a little, he tries a little joke . . . ("See? The dead do rise.)

And Alice is in.

She frightens Browne, and her resurrection suggests that scarier people still may have returned.

He dispenses with the formalities ("You look ferocious . . ."), and asks what's really worrying him ("Is *he* [father] here, too?"). Browne tries to reassure himself ("But no, I suppose he couldn't be."), but it's too menacing and that face was too real ("The silk merchant.").

Her incredulity offends and frightens Browne—he doesn't want to be going mad, seeing things. So he tries a little pleasant exchange ("Does convent life agree with you, Alice? Not too quiet?").

Even composing a little ditty for her (". . . Into the sea poor Alice was tossed . . .") as he did when Alice and he were children.

But she's still there, *wanting* something. It's too terrifying. He begins worrying about the silk merchant again, and he talks to silence her voice, to not listen to this demanding . . . *But* talking about the silk merchant makes Browne remember that he is as his father was when he died.

Alice talks again. Browne turns away from her, he tells her about the writing desk and how the faces of the dead terrify him, how *her* face is terrifying to him.

And still she won't go. She too wants the Will. Browne decides to evict her.

He tells her everything there is to tell about himself, beginning with his wife (who is getting all the money), and ends by telling Alice that she is hurting him, explicitly asking her to go ("Your presence is too vital and it causes pain.").

It enrages Browne that Alice won't leave after he tells her this, that she is still after the one thing she came to get, the Will, the money. He blasts her ("There's a distinctly mercenary scent . . .").

It works, she starts to leave, but Browne is afraid. Can she help him?

She can't and doesn't.

She leaves. Maybe the holy water will help, so he drinks it.

Babbo announces the arrival of a foreigner, and Browne knows who it is. He expects Estrelita, but Dorothy enters. He finds her presence reassuring ("Not so foreign after all."). After all is said and done, Browne knows his wife and she knows him.

Maccabbee too reassures him, familiar. Browne gives Macc his marching orders, sends him off, and prepares to meet the next visitor who has come to say good-bye—Estrelita.

But Dorothy tells Browne she's brought the gravedigger. This is a betrayal. But also what he asked for. He attacks her with considerable nastiness, in front of Pumpkin, and after she flees, Browne feels badly, he even admits to his misbehavior in front of this upstart, this usurper, and the usurper throws down a gauntlet. ("Yes, sir. I do.")

Browne realizes that Pumpkin's ready to fight. Browne chooses to fight by giving Pumpkin this list of impossible contradictory orders: do this, but not that! This, and not that! Browne uses the words, the surprising twists, the paradoxes of the speech about burial to stab at him; he becomes flush with the victory, which he imagines his verbal dexterity, his talent, is giving him. He flings false modesty at Pumpkin, he flings his sins at Pumpkin (". . . who made his wife miserable . . ."), his failure to have grandchildren—BUT (a hairpin turn) HE IS A GENIUS! SHAKESPEARE HAD NOTHING ON HIM! He deserves AN OBELISK! A PYRAMID! A PYRE! A GRAND SEA BURIAL . . .

HE IS THE CENTER OF THE UNIVERSE, and he cannot die! The idea is preposterous! Everything, even this wretch, depends on him and his continued life! He will never die. He dismisses the possibility, and for a moment feels immortal, victorious ("We'll have no need of gravediggers then!").

But as soon as Pumpkin starts to talk back, and even worse, to walk, healthy, young . . . Browne can only hope to hurt Dorothy through Pumpkin by saying, "Tell her I died *knowing*." He wants her to know that she hurt him terribly.

And then he takes that back. There are several meanings to: "No, don't tell her anything."—leave her with nothing, just silence, leave them all with that, or possibly Browne has decided not to hurt her; or possibly he means both.

Estrelita's visit is painful, and also redemptive: she has loved him all this time, in spite of his having been a coward, of his having abandond her, all things Browne has spent his life despising himself for. She never stopped loving him, and she promises to take him home with her.

Estrelita's visit completes the stations Browne has had to visit on his way to what he believes is a truce he's made with dying. The last interruption of the eulogies is dispensed with easily, with magisterial calm—he wants to be alone, with Dorothy, to try to face the end.

They are embarrassed to be together. He is moved by her loyalty, she is frightened that he is clearly near the end; they are sad that there is so much hatred between them, her betrayal of him, his cruelty to her. He confesses to his role in the killing of the women accused of witchcraft—the memory of their hanging has never left him; the guilt he has suffered, he who is essentially a decent man, has been an awful torment.

He drifts, slowly letting go, the toxins inside overwhelming him. He has a final vision ("Dorothy, good-bye. The ship embarks at first wind. The mast and sails are gilded with blood . . ."), which is also his farewell to the world, his final poem. She loses her nerve at the end, and cannot wait to watch him breathe his last; she runs away to find help, and Father Death finally makes his move. Browne begs for his life, tries to move this monster to pity, tries reproaches, pleas, but . . .

BOOM BOOM BOOM.

Act Five

When Browne comes back from the Other Side to deliver his Will, he is hungry, vibrant, joyous, mobile, feeling great for the first time in years. He is also an instrument of Vengeance, and is enjoying that, the delivering of Justice, immensely.

G. David Schine in Hell

With apologies to George Bernard Shaw,
Philip Roth, God, the Devil
and everyone in between

Cast

G. DAVID SCHINE

ROY COHN

ALGER HESS

DICK

MARY

Setting

Hell, June 19, 1996

We are in Hell—Have you noticed?—which resembles a dinner theater in Orange County, California, across the interstate from the Nixon Library. Onstage are four music stands placed before four bar stools, on each of which a man is sitting. Three are dressed elegantly in black tuxedos, and the fourth, Roy Cohn, is wearing tuxedo pants and an aggressively busy, plaid red-green-heather-mustard dinner jacket, with matching bow tie and cummerbund. Roy turns to the Elderly Gentleman seated next to him.

ROY

Come here often? What's your sign?

ELDERLY GENTLEMAN

My . . . ?

ROY

Scorpio? Cancer? What're you drinking?

ELDERLY GENTLEMAN

I'm not . . . *(A glass appears in his hand, yellowish ice, parasol, pineapple chunk on a toothpick)* Oh! *(He sips it)* Banana daiquiri?

(Roy sticks his finger in the man's drink, licks, makes a face.)

ROY

Bleah. I knew a guy who drank that dreck by the bucket—his dad owned a hotel in Boca Raton. The bartender claimed he'd *invented* the banana daiquiri and, oh yeah, there was this gal down there who'd marry wealthy old diabetics, get them hooked on banana daiquiris and—

ELDERLY GENTLEMAN

(Recognizing Roy) Oh my God, it's . . .

ROY

What?

ELDERLY GENTLEMAN

Where . . . Where am I?

ROY

In Hell. *(Staring at the man more intently)* What did you say your name was?

ELDERLY GENTLEMAN

I didn't say, I . . . *HELL?* No, but that's not . . . Roy?

ROY

Don't I know you from some . . .

ELDERLY GENTLEMAN

Roy Cohn?

ROY

David? David Schine?

DAVID

ROY COHN! This *must* be Hell!

(They hug.)

ROY

Dave, Dave, so great to see you, look! *(Wipes his eyes)* Tears! So *old*, Dave!

DAVID

But what am I doing here? There's a mistake somewhere, Roy, I've been really good, the last fifty years, I mean, not *perfect*, but

I produced a hit movie! I married Miss Universe! I should be in Heaven, Roy.

ROY

Oh, you'd hate Heaven, Dave, trust me.

DAVID

I do, Roy.

ROY

You always did. Incredible.

DAVID

But what's so bad about Heaven, Roy?

ROY

Fulla kvetchy communists, Dave, trying to figure out how the Great Leap Forward turned into the Biggest Bellyflop in History. Bill Kunstler's up there, for God's sake. Trust me, Hell's better.

DAVID

Who's in Hell?

ROY

All Republicans, many Democrats, Jesse Helms—I know, he's not really dead but he has a backstage pass. Whittaker Chambers with that fekachteh medal Reagan gave him. Buy him a drink and he'll polish it on your necktie.

DAVID

What about Purgatory?

ROY

Lionel Trilling, and the editorial board of the *New York Review of Books*. Nobody ever gave *me* a medal. Ingrates.

DAVID

Naw, Roy, they all hate you up there, pretty much everyone except Bill Buckley. And they say you were a fag.

ROY

Bisexual! Please! And so was Whittaker!

DAVID

But I tell 'em it just isn't true, Roy, you were a ladies' man.

ROY

Dave, Dave, such a sweet, simple kid. Hey, but listen kiddo, here you don't have to look like an alter kocher anymore, here you're spirit, not flesh—in Hell you can look any age you want!

DAVID

But you didn't change, Roy, you look sixty.

ROY

What are you kidding, *change*? After I paid for all these face-lifts? Oh alright I *didn't* actually *pay* for them, but I think I look better now than I did then, and anyway, as the very Embodiment or rather as the Spirit of American Conservatism—you know, the unconsidered contradictions, the ill-considered unconstitutional adventurism, the paranoia, the ebullient bile—I *can't* change, it wouldn't look good. You on the other hand don't have a political bone in your body, Dave, so let me see you again as the gorgeous rich boy for whose sake I nearly sank the anticommunist movement! The face that launched a thousand slips!

DAVID

OK, Roy!

(Whisk! He changes into a twenty-five year old—handsome in his GI uniform.)

ROY

There you are! Poetry is what you drive me to! The dreams I've had of you, Dave—of us, of our schtupping and caressing, of our World-purging love! You, a nice Jewish boy I could bring home to my mother—alright so maybe not a genius, but with a face and a body like the replacement lead in a Tarzan movie! *And* a hotel chain and a bank account!

DAVID

Roy, Roy, *such* a kidder.

ROY

Who's kidding? Even *you* must have known, you must have suspected. For *you* I ruined the credibility and career of the man I admired most in all the world, for your sake I pushed Joe McCarthy to perdition, Dave—for you—because Joe had moxie like nobody's business but he didn't have your eyes! Dave, our story is epic, it's tragic, it's . . . *South Pacific.* Dave, my doomed love for you turned you into history—Dave, you gotta know that! And what about that afternoon we spent in that hotel in Munich?

DAVID

Aw, Roy, that was 1952—who remembers? And I had serious jet lag in Munich, you know that, and my cold medicine made me sorta dopey. I loved you too, guy, like my vicious kid brother or something, such a cutup! I was real sad when I read you'd gotten sick and died from—

ROY

Liver cancer.

DAVID

Oh, right, liver . . . But I thought the papers said it was—well, never mind. But *history*, Roy, gee, I dunno, I mean, you sure got my name in all the papers, Roy, you sure did, but no one reads the papers anymore, the kids these days, all that stuff is pretty much forgotten. You, me, Senator Joe, all that. Nobody remembers *last month*, let alone 1952.

(Music plays: "The Internationale." Spotlight on the third man, who looks around as if waiting for someone.)

DAVID

Roy, who's—

ROY

Hiss, David.

(David hisses.)

DAVID

Why are we hissing, Roy? Is it the Devil?

ROY

No, no you lamebrain, it's Alger Hiss.

DAVID

(Not remembering the name) Alger . . . ?

ROY

Oh for christ sake!

ALGER

Microfilm in the pumpkin?

DAVID

OH RIGHT! Jeez, I haven't thought about you in years! But, Roy, you said all the commies were up in—

ROY

He visits.

ALGER

Change of scenery, that sort of thing. Thinking of relocating.

DAVID

You mean that's possible?

ALGER

To switch? Of course, old man, didn't they teach you that at Harvard?

ROY

He wasn't an A student.

ALGER

I suppose not. Yes, anyone can switch and Lord knows many do. I come down here for a little moral *certainty*, you know, even if it's obtained at the price of an appalling degree of moral shortsightedness, here at least you know who you are. Up there everyone's swimming in guilt, ideological confusion, and the *questions*, my God! "Did you do it, Alger?" "You never did it, did you, Alger?" "Why did you do it, Alger?" "But what about the Hitler-Stalin anti-aggression pact, Alger?" "Were we *wrong*, Alger?" Right, like *I* know the answer! Do I look like Teresias?

DAVID

Who?

ALGER

Teresias. A Greek androgyne, Mr. Schine, he had breasts.

DAVID

Communist?

ALGER

I should think so, yes.

ROY

Here at least we know you, Alger. Even if you never spied (which you *did*), you organized the UN. For that alone you shoulda done time.

ALGER

And don't forget Yalta!

(The wailing of the Damned.)

ALGER

I love this place! In Heaven it's all soul-searching. Here in Hell you haven't got any souls to search, and it's still possible for a man to produce an *effect*.
So you fellows really were queers, huh, it wasn't just gossip?

ROY

Never take the name of Gossip in vain, especially down here—it's the brandy of the damned.

ALGER

You stole that line from Shaw.

ROY

Oh yeah, like *I* ever read that Fabian socialist windbag.
Are you looking for someone in particular?

ALGER

An old comrade of mine. He lives here, we're going to discuss trading apartments. He's late, he—

(Music: "Hail to the Chief." Spotlight on the fourth man, immediately recognizable by the jowls, the ski-slope nose, the widow's peak hairline, the alarming nervous grin.)

DICK

Sorry, I was finishing the seventy-fifth volume of my memoirs and geopolitical stratagems. Just because I'm dead doesn't mean I have to stop writing.

ALGER

You should be punctual.

DICK

Too many (expletive deleted) meetings. Too many (expletive deleted) GOP ideologues, hounding me, hounding me. "Dick, you were never a *true* conservative." "Dick, you were (expletive deleted) Leonid Brezhnev." Wage-and-Price-Control-Dick, they call me—last of the tax-and-spend liberals: "Ten steps to the left of Bill (expletive deleted) Clinton." I hate it here! I have always been a . . . a *thinker*! I want to go to Heaven, where people still believe in government. I want some (expletive deleted) respect.

ALGER

But you know, Dick, they despise you up there.

DICK

Yeah, well sticks and stones and (expletive deleted).

ROY

We hate him down here, too. The man's entirely devoid of charm. He's hated everywhere. It's a talent he has.

DICK

Bob Dole likes me. And the rest of you can go (expletive deleted) yourselves. Heaven is all (inaudible) and (expletive deleted) (expletive deleted), but at least I can hope for some intelligent conversation. I—Oh, what the (expletive deleted) is it *now*?

(The "Glinda" entrance music is heard. A bubble with an oily iridescent sheen descends from the lighting grid. Out steps a dumpy man with a face like a Walt Kelly bulldog, wearing a black Chanel dress, hose and stiletto pumps on which he teeters uncertainly.)

DICK

And that's another thing I hate about this place! The gender confusion!

ALGER

I'm with you on that one, Dick, but it's *worse* in Heaven!

ROY

Dave, may I present: The Son of the New Morning! Mary!

DAVID

It looks like J. Edgar Hoover, Roy.

EDGAR

Hello, Girls! Heard there was a new arrival, thought it might be Arthur Finkelstein.

DAVID

Roy, I'm real confused.

EDGAR

Of course you are, beautiful.

ROY

You always were . . .

AND IT GOES ON

Notes on Akiba

This is of course for Michael Mayer—
my best girlfriend, who else?

Notes on Akiba was performed at The Jewish Museum's Third Seder on April 13, 1995, in New York City. Neil Goldberg, Joan Hocky and Alicia Suigals were the Producers, Aviva Weintraub was the Program Director, Karen Sherman was the Stage Manager, Allessandro Cavadini was the Technical Director and Troy Matthews provided technical support. The piece was read by Tony Kushner (Michael) and Michael Mayer (Tony).

Author's Note

The historical information contained in this piece comes from a variety of sources, my usual rabbinate: Bloom, Scholem, Yerushalmi, Steinsaltz; and an important new guest at the table, Ira Steingroot. Everything factual in the piece, indeed everything you could ever want to know about Passover, can be found in Steingroot's remarkable, indispensable, delightful and erudite *Keeping Passover*, published by Harper Collins.

This piece is exegesis, not autobiography. My father does not skip, he is a menschlakh elaborator. He is praiseworthy.

Many thanks to Norman Kleeblatt and The Jewish Museum, and especially to The Klezmatics for including this in their Third Seder, on the occasion of which this was written.

Two gay Jewish men, Michael, in his mid-thirties, and Tony, forty, sit at a table, facing each other. They are making charoset: chopped nuts, apples, spice and wine. The table is covered with the ingredients: just-peeled apples, the peels strewn about; piles of shelled nuts; a bottle of Schapiro's Extra Heavy Malaga, Kosher for Passover ("Wine So Thick You Can Cut It with a Knife!"); ginger root; cinnamon; cardamom; cloves; a jar of honey. There are knives, two chopping boards and a big heavy bowl into which the chopped ingredients are placed. There are also two large green leeks on the table, and a box of matzoh.
They turn to the audience.)

TONY

This is Michael Mayer.

MICHAEL

This is Tony Kushner. These are notes on Akiba. This is exegesis, or, elaboration.

(As they talk, they chop.)

TONY

OK OK let me begin by apologizing, OK, so I wrote this in a hurry so I wrote this in haste so I wrote this on the fly on a fucking *AIRPLANE* I wrote this so it's not funny so it makes no sense so it doesn't work so don't laugh so don't come so sue me it's not like anyone's *paying* me to do this, not like anyone's *paying* me to do this and *HIM*, he never saw the script before an hour ago, so forget memorizing it he is totally confused but the haste is appropriate, the airline is appropriate, I travel too much,

my father was a wandering Aramaean, alright, so sue me, WHAT ARE YOU DOING HERE ANYWAY don't you have company coming tomorrow night shouldn't you be at home now on your hands and knees scouring for Chametz DID YOU GET EVERY CRUMB *ARE YOU SURE?* HE is not responsible for this the Klezmatics are not responsible for this the clarinetist is so hot he reminds me of my father shouldn't you be at home cooking for your father don't you have company have a family have friends have a father coming over what are you an animal or something I worry about you don't get hurt don't get shot drive safely wear a condom I alone am responsible I alone bear responsibility I cannot bear the responsibility it is insupportable it is impossible it is imponderable.
This, by way of prologue.

(Pause.
They chop apples and nuts.)

MICHAEL
In some Sefardic Seders the celebrants lash each other with leeks.

(They lash each other with leeks.)

TONY
Ow.

MICHAEL
They do this because in the desert the people complained to Moses, missing the fish and onions they enjoyed eating in Egypt. The leek lashing is to remind them that there is a high price to pay for tasty things sometimes. The price for fish and leeks in Egypt was the lash. The Passover practice, in coastal villages of the Mediterranean, of lashing each other with fish, died out by the fourth century C.E.; Hellenizing influences are credited with the eventual replacement of fish whips with the more manageable leek.
The more one elaborates.

TONY

Elaborates. E-LAB-OR-ATES. *Elaborates.*

MICHAEL

On the departure from Egypt the more praiseworthy one is.

(They chop.)

TONY

But my father skipped it.

MICHAEL

Everyone does.

TONY

So I said to him, you skip it!

MICHAEL

Everyone does.

TONY

Every year. Right after the Four Questions. Do the Four Questions and then start the story and then you get to that bit and then, SKIP.

MICHAEL

The Fier Kashe.

(Pause.)

TONY

Right.

MICHAEL

I like saying the Hebrew. *Fier Kashe.* The delicious nasalities, the slides, the wide open vowel sounds, the abrupt syncopation.

TONY

They skip it because it's like, oh, it's like one of those medieval Jewish numerological things, one of those . . . *(Gestures)*

MICHAEL

Every letter has a value.

TONY

So he said of course he said I don't skip it.

MICHAEL

Oh bullshit.

TONY

But he does. Who doesn't? Everyone does.

MICHAEL

"Echad," the Hebrew word for "One," has letters the numerological value of which add up to thirteen: hence the thirteen verses in the game that begins, "Who knows one," hence, "Who knows thirteen I know thirteen thirteen are God's attributes etc."

TONY

These attributes, by the way, what are they?

MICHAEL

They are immensely potent emenatory demi-divine entities suffused throughout the world of prayerful visionary journeying as mystical lights as described in Kaballah, Jewish magic.

TONY

A nervy thing to invoke at the tail end of what is let's face it a children's counting game.

MICHAEL

We read in the Zohar that—

TONY

But what really makes my gorge rise is that he can't *admit* he skips the whole, you know, that part that bit that Tarphon that whatsisname . . .

MICHAEL

Akiba.

TONY

Right, Akiba, *that* bit which everyone skips because it's like who knows what it's about so like what is the big fucking deal about skipping it. I've only been going to his Seder for forty years practically and I like think I would know if he skips it or not and believe me *he skips it* but what's *sick* is that he can't admit he skips it because you know why? Because his *FATHER* never skipped anything not one part not one bit not one word of Hebrew every word, every detour and digression, with his father they would sit for hours and hours the Seder would take hours, and he of course cannot is like *molecularly* incapable of conceiving that he maybe does *less* than his *FATHER* did because it's like Jewish men, it's this sick thing, isn't it, it's this sick thing, this sick sick sick sick sick thing they have with their fathers, all Jewish men have it or is it all men period or is it just me? It's sick. I told him that.

MICHAEL

What?

TONY

That it's sick, sick, a crazy competitive . . . and—

MICHAEL

What did he say?

TONY

He said, "It's . . . That's a sick thing to say to your father." But. I mean really, like, *out of the house of bondage*, right?

MICHAEL

Totally.

TONY

I mean *please*.

(Pause.
They put the chopped apples and nuts in the bowl.
Michael adds spices while talking.)

MICHAEL

A favorite Passover treat of Jewish American kids of the '30s, '40s and '50s was to break up matzoh crackers, remember when we used to call them matzoh crackers, my family did—anyway I grew up in Maryland—was to break up matzoh crackers into a bowl and cover the broken pieces with condensed milk and Fox's U-Bet Syrup and then with a fork you mash the pieces and the condensed milk and syrup into a sticky lavender-gray gluten, a paste. This paste represents the bricking mortar Jews in Mizrayim made *with* straw *before* Pharaoh took the straw away, punitively, and then mortar had to be made *without* straw, which is charoset. The matzoh represents the pious deflation of the pridefulness of man and woman as they approach God during this Holy Week of Remembrance, not puffed up with the yeast of their pretensions and their vainglories. Flat. Broken up in pieces in a bowl, the matzoh means basically the same thing as it does whole, in a box. The condensed milk is known as the Milk of Affliction. It represents canned food, the food of haste, of fallout shelters, especially in the '50s and early '60s. The meaning of Fox's U-Bet Syrup is obscure. It is not a traditional component of *Shulchan Arukh*, the Prepared Table.

(They chop again.)

TONY

Do you think what I said is like self-hating, the sick thing part, is that—

MICHAEL

No. I mean it's not necessarily true, but it—

TONY

Oh, it's *true.* It is *true.* It's just maybe also it's self-hating, I worry about that because, I love Passover I really do but it's my family. You skip you don't elaborate you don't quibble you don't haggle you don't explicate or enumerate or niggle or nit-pick, you hasten through the hard parts, you go right from the questions and then skip over these tired old men, who cares about tired old men lets get to the kids, the young people, the wise one and the wicked and the gornisht slow one and the one who knows not what to ask. For whom, specifically, copious elaboration is salutary. But who gets short shrift while everyone is guiltily aware that wedged into this crack between the Questions and The Story and The Kids, between the easy, folksy bits, the stuff about kids that's basically only in there to keep the kids from sliding under the table or keep them awake or not kicking up fusses because they don't really care about the Exodus, "for you and not for me," right, that's kids, what do kids care about but *kids*, right, so over the centuries you learn to stick in all this stuff about kids so they stay awake and don't fidget and you can schlepp nakhes—

MICHAEL

Schepp.

TONY

What?

MICHAEL

You *schepp* nakhes, you *schlepp* . . . other things.

(Pause.)

TONY

... And, and look how good my kid is he ... *performs*, he really *performs*, he *memorizes*, he is *prepared*, a *performer*, he's four years old he can barely read *Green Eggs and Ham* and look he has memorized lengthy strings of what are to him nonsense syllables which he will now produce flawlessly on command because he knows like *the whole year to follow and his life along with it will be cursed, the crops will fail and Elijah won't come because YOU FORGOT WHAT COMES AFTER MA NISHTANAH ETCETERA,* and like that's not affliction?

(Pause.
Then they put the chopped nuts and apples in the bowl.
Michael adds spices.)

MICHAEL

There are fifteen verses to *Dayenu*. One verse each for each of the steps that led up to the door of the First Temple. Hence the song's ladder-like structure. Passover songs appeal to children primarily through games of simple mastery, building, accumulating, accelerating, challenges to reading proficiency and lung capacity.

(As they talk, they add honey and spices, and they taste.)

TONY

So now we are going to read and do exegesis on the part everybody skips. "A tale is told of Rabbi Eleazar—

MICHAEL

Eleazar ben Hyrcanus, first and second centuries a Mishnaic sage, a tanna, teacher of Akiba.

TONY

Rabbi Joshua—

MICHAEL

A creator of Post-Temple Judaism. They all were, actually, the ones who survived.

TONY

Rabbi Eleazar ben Azariah—

MICHAEL

Named head of the Sanhedrin when he was eighteen.

TONY

Rabbi Akiba—

MICHAEL

Didn't survive. The greatest Mishnaic Tannaim of them all. When Moses was receiving the Commandments from God on Sinai he asked God why there were all the little curlicues on Hebrew letters, the points and the thorns and God said, "Turn around," and Moses did and lo, he was looking, two thousand years in the future, looking through a window into Rabbi Akiba's yeshiva in Bene-Berak, and Akiba was doing exegesis on the five books of Moses which Moses of course had yet to write, and Moses turned back around again and God said, "That man Akiba is so smart he will be able to interpret even the curlicues on the letters of the words of the books you will someday write."

TONY

Rabbi Tarphon.

MICHAEL

Also didn't survive. His two most famous sayings are: "The day is short the task is great the workers are lazy the reward is much the Master is insistent."

TONY

And he also said: "The task cannot be completed by you, but neither are you free to desist from the task."

MICHAEL

This is from the Haggadah: "A tale is told of Rabbi Eleazar and Rabbi Joshua and Rabbi Eleazar ben Azariah and Rabbi Akiba and Rabbi Tarphon who reclined together at Bene-Berak. And they recounted the departure from Egypt all night until their students came to them and said, "Masters, the time has come to recite the morning Shema."

Said Rabbi Eleazar ben Azariah, "I am like unto a man seventy years old . . ." This is because his hair had turned white prematurely when, at the age of eighteen, he was made head of the Sanhedrin, and so he was "like" a seventy year old but actually much younger.

TONY

He is the wise son. I am the wicked son.

MICHAEL

"I am like unto a man seventy years old, yet I never found biblical proof as to why the Exodus from Egypt should be recited in the evening service until ben Zoma . . ."

TONY

Elaborate, be praiseworthy.

MICHAEL

ben Zoma, a Jewish mystic who went to Heaven and lost his mind as a result—

TONY

The thirteen attributes, no doubt.

MICHAEL

Possibly.

TONY

Go on.

MICHAEL

. . . Explained the verse, "So that you may remember the day of your departure from the land of Egypt all the days of your life." (Deuteronomy, chapter 16 verse 3): "The days of your life" implies the daytime while, "All the days of your life," implies the nights. And the sages amplify this by saying, "The days of your life," refers to this world; "All the days of your life," to Messianic times as well.

And now we will perform an exegesis on the traditional lack of exegesis concerning this passage.

TONY

The reason people skip over this hardly lengthy section has something to do, I think, at least on the surface, with the tension set up in the form of the Seder between the forward-moving motional urgency of appetite, on the one hand, and the profound reluctance on the other hand of true critical thought to move ahead. Wait, wait, there is more to glean, there is always more. Also, everyone has stored up in her or his actual memory or probably after three or four thousand years of Seders probably stored in your genetic memory are nightmare Seders of days gone by when fathers and sons competed for the honor of being most praiseworthy, elaborating and prolonging as these rabbis did till Dawn.

(They add the Schapiro's Kosher Wine.)

MICHAEL

The rabbis who nobody wants to hear from anymore return in the Haggadah a second time in the plague section.

TONY

Counting the fingers and the fingerbones of God.

MICHAEL

Multiplying plagues. 260 plagues. 400 plagues. In this way exalting the Miracle of Liberation.

TONY

This bit is also skipped over.

MICHAEL

Because it is lengthy, confusing, too close to dinner to be endured, and exceedingly bloodcurdling.

(Tony stirs the ingredients.)

TONY

It contains a Ten Plagues mnemonic, Detzakh Adash Beahab. The letters of which contain the first letters of the Ten Plagues. Detzakh Adash Beahab translates literally, "A scorpion bit my uncle."

MICHAEL

This ancient mnemonic apparently inspired Jewish communities in North Africa and in Tijuana Mexico to compose a Pesach counting song, "A Scorpion Bit My Uncle," but the traditional song has been largely abandoned in this century, due to the arrival of modern insecticides and a concomitant lessening of the anxieties provoked by the mnemonic. In countries to which the scorpion is not indigenous, the song never caught on.

TONY

This fear of skipping, of cheating, of eliding, effacing, passing over with many a secret sigh of relief the imponderably weighty inheritance of millennia of Jewish intellectual, theological, political, historical, mystical *effort*. The imponderability creating as symptom the desire to skip.

MICHAEL

The propensity to skip.

TONY

Yes.

MICHAEL

Gracefully, but guiltily.

TONY

Yes.

MICHAEL

I know what you mean. The elegant uneasy skip of the dilettante. The, "I don't need to know that," as opposed to the injunction, "Know everything, know it all. Even the curlicues: Know them." Be praiseworthy.

TONY

Which symptom producing the ache of insufficiency. The tribal genetically encoded Darwinian anxiety of inexorable decline down through the generations, the entropic cooling down unto Death.

MICHAEL

And hence of course how perfect that what we skip is this brief odd strobic glimpse of these particular five men, these Protean daddies, their massive hairy forearms, wound tightly, perhaps even a little cruelly, with the leather phylactery straps, their bulky foreheads bound and bearing boxes enshrining tiny curled-up parchment leaves representing leaves of flame upon which are inscribed letters of flame representing words and sounds which are the dark crackle of midnight-devouring Holy Fire. Tented with tallises, fringy with tzitzits. Reclining. On pillows. Talking and singing through the night.

TONY

That is too elaborate. Perhaps.

MICHAEL

Talking about the Exodus. What has passed. How the future is to receive it. How to carry the imponderable burden of it.

TONY

Judaism has as a distinguishing feature its unreasonable difficulty. It is unappeasably hard. You must remember. You must remember everything. You must write down what you remember. You must read what you have written every year. Not once a year but for a whole week. And even worse you must *understand.* And even worse you must *elaborate* on that understanding.

MICHAEL

The freeing of the slave only commences the wandering of the now-homeless. The freed slave is still unfree. Only after his arrival in some safe shelter is the freed slave free. The Exodus is also an affliction.

(They pour each other a glass of Extra Heavy Malaga.)

TONY

A woman in the town I grew up in searched her house the night before Pesach with a candle searching out the Chametz as is traditional, and she made a big pile of crumbs but forgot to burn them and left the unburned Chametz in the dustpan in the utility closet and maybe it's a coincidence but from her chicken soup, which she thought the room was cold enough to let stand outside the refrigerator overnight because the refrigerator was full of kugel and whatnot and so everyone at the Seder table the next night got botulism and had to go to the emergency room.

MICHAEL

Why is this night different from all other nights? On all other nights gay Jewish men are channeling their mothers. On this night gay Jewish men are channeling their great-great-grandmothers from the Russian Pale.

The rabbis reclining at Bene-Berak that we skip over in the Haggadah are plotting rebellion against the Roman Empire.

Perhaps instead of recounting the Exodus as they are supposed to have been doing they are working out strategies of resistance. This garrison is weak, that one is vulnerably positioned, we might roll big stones off the tops of those cliffs and bash in the skull of that centurion, this captain, that governor. Is Death a part of the miracle that brings liberation?

TONY

For instance God Forgive me God Forgive me, but how is Senator D'Amato doing with those chest pains?

MICHAEL

Perhaps the young students rushing in in the story to warn the rabbis that day has arrived are speaking in code. Perhaps, "Hear Oh Israel," in this instance means, "Put away the maps, the Romans are nearby." This is conjecture and so inappropriate as elaboration. Akiba declared Bar Kochba Messiah and commenced the rebellion.

TONY

Bar Kochba is slain.

MICHAEL

And Akiba is tortured and slain.

TONY

And the Temple is destroyed and the Diaspora begins. A condition of permanent Exodus.

MICHAEL

A liberation and also an affliction. In some Haggadahs the Akiba section ends with a quadruple benediction: The Place, God, The Torah, God. Ha-Makon, Hebrew for "The place," is one of God's many names.

TONY

Towards which perhaps we are wandering.

(Pause.
They taste the charoset.)

TONY

I apologize for my earlier fit of pique. It's the stress, the stress, I'm under a lot of stress.

MICHAEL

Who isn't?

TONY

We all are.

MICHAEL

We are.

TONY

Blessed is The Place. Blessed is God, giver of The Torah. Blessed is The Torah. Blessed is God.

MICHAEL

H'ag Sameach.

(They toast each other, and drink wine.)

END

Terminating

OR

Sonnet LXXV

OR

"Lass meine Schmerzen nicht verloren sein"

OR

Ambivalence

This play is for
Deborah Glazer, Ph.D.

Terminating was produced by The Acting Company (New York City) in association with the Guthrie Theater Lab (Minneapolis) on January 7, 1998 as part of "Love's Fire," an evening of plays inspired by Shakespeare's sonnets. Mark Lamos was the director, Michael Yeargan was the scenic designer, Candice Donnelly was the costume designer, Robert Wierzel was the lighting designer and John Gromada was the sound designer. The cast was as follows:

ESTHER	Erika Rolfsrud
HENDRYK	Stephen DeRosa
DYMPHNA	Lisa Tharps
BILLYGOAT	Hamish Linklater

Thanks to Mark Lamos, who asked me to do this, always a wild joy to work with. Thanks to my sister, Lesley Kushner, for her generosity regarding my primitive (writer's) capital accumulation.

Characters

ESTHER, an analyst, early thirties

HENDRYK, a former patient of Esther's, early thirties

DYMPHNA, Esther's lover/domestic partner/spousal equivalent, late twenties

BILLYGOAT, Hendryk's soon-to-be ex-boyfriend, early thirties

Place

Esther's office on the Upper West Side, New York City

So are you to my thoughts as food to life,
Or as sweet seasoned showers are to the ground;
And for the peace of you I hold such strife
As 'twixt a miser and his wealth is found:
Now proud as an enjoyer, and anon
Doubting the filching age will steal his treasure;
Now counting best to be with you alone,
Then bettered that the world might see my pleasure:
Sometime all full with feasting on your sight,
And by and by clean-starved for a look;
Possessing or pursuing no delight
Save what is had, or must from you be took.
Thus do I pine, and surfeit day by day,
Or gluttoning on all, or all away.

Sonnet LXXV

—SHAKESPEARE

Esther is an analyst, and this is her office. Hendryk sits *on the couch, he does not* lie *on the couch. Esther and Hendryk are roughly the same age. Esther is nicely turned out, Hendryk is a godforsaken mess. Dymphna, Esther's younger domestic partner, sits in a chair near Esther. Billygoat, Hendryk's erstwhile much-more-attractive lover, sits near the couch.*

HENDRYK

I've gained twenty-four pounds.

ESTHER

Hendryk.

HENDRYK

Last night on the subway I urinated.

ESTHER

Hendryk.

HENDRYK

In my pants.

ESTHER

Hendryk.

HENDRYK

Bladder, um, bladder control, loss of, sudden loss of . . . Waters breaking, whoosh! Drenched!

ESTHER

Hendryk.

HENDRYK

I'm broke.

ESTHER

Hendryk.

HENDRYK

I spent all my money on these . . . these . . . these . . .

ESTHER

Hendryk.

HENDRYK

I . . . *(He waits for the "Hendryk." It doesn't come)*
I, I didn't *need* them, it was just, they're . . . Drapes. It was an idea I had, to, to sew real, uh real, uh *actual* chicken feathers—

ESTHER

Hendryk.

HENDRYK

. . . Quilted, sort of, big squares between sheets of sheer, um, *raw* . . . silk.
(He waits for the "Hendryk." It doesn't come so he says) Hendryk. I find I'm saying *raw* a lot these days, raw silk, raw . . . um, burlap steak wound meat eat me raw the, the raw truth. Raw and, um, *rank.* Rank . . . *betrayal.*

ESTHER

Hen—

HENDRYK

All this coil is long of you. Mistress. As they say. *RAW.* Not like I'm not perfectly contented to be free of this room and the constraints of your ultimate indifference to the, uh, the uhhhhh, the.

(Pause.)

ESTHER

Hendryk.

HENDRYK

I want to come back.

ESTHER

No.

HENDRYK

Why not?

ESTHER

I—

HENDRYK

Why?

ESTHER

We terminated.

HENDRYK

So?

ESTHER

You . . .
Because.

HENDRYK

What?

ESTHER

You frighten me.

HENDRYK

You're not supposed to say things like that. You're not supposed to say anything, really.

ESTHER

I can say anything I want, Hendryk, you're not my patient anymore.

HENDRYK

But still.

ESTHER

Well you do frighten me.

HENDRYK

I am in love with you.

ESTHER

Transference.

HENDRYK

I don't believe in transference.

ESTHER

Uh-huh.

HENDRYK

All love is transference. Breast, mom, every fucking other fucking—

ESTHER

Hendryk.

HENDRYK

I love you.

ESTHER

Hendryk, you do not, I mean—

HENDRYK

I do. It's not—

ESTHER

Hendryk, I—

HENDRYK

. . . transference.

ESTHER

I HAVE PROBLEMS OF MY OWN, HENDRYK! PROBLEMS! PROBLEMS!

DYMPHNA

I thought you terminated with him. Tell him to leave. Is it bad today?

HENDRYK

This isn't going well and perhaps I should . . .

(Pause.)

ESTHER

I should not have said that you frighten me.

HENDRYK

Countertransference.

ESTHER

Well . . .

HENDRYK

Unanalyzed countertransference.

(Pause.)

HENDRYK

What?

ESTHER

It . . .

HENDRYK

Oh. It's . . . *not* counter . . . So, it's . . . what? *Reality?*

ESTHER

Hendryk.

HENDRYK

I *am*, I mean I actually *am* . . . *Frightening*? I mean, *me*?

(Pause.)

HENDRYK

I. Um. The. Um. A-ha. A . . . ha. Wow.

ESTHER

How would it make you feel if I said you were frightening?

HENDRYK

But you did say that.

ESTHER

And how did—

HENDRYK

No if.

ESTHER

But how—

HENDRYK

No hypothetical.

ESTHER

But.

HENDRYK

You *said* it.
Sleep with me. At least.

ESTHER

(Laughs) You're gay.

HENDRYK

Oh yeah, well, so what. Gay. What. Is. That. You're a dyke, I'm gay, so—

ESTHER

Actually I never said I was a—

HENDRYK

Oh come on.

ESTHER

What?

HENDRYK

You wear . . . *Harley Davidson boots* and you have short hair.

ESTHER

Once I wore those boots.

HENDRYK

We saw each other for—

ESTHER

You were my patient.

HENDRYK

I . . . what?

ESTHER

We didn't "see" each other.

HENDRYK

For five years.

ESTHER

You make it sound like we dated.

HENDRYK

You think this is all about my mother.

ESTHER

It's not *not* about your mother. Of course I think it's about—

HENDRYK

I think you're a dyke.

ESTHER

Lesbian.

HENDRYK

Wasn't hostile.

ESTHER

Felt like it.

DYMPHNA

(To Esther) Thought he was gone.

ESTHER

(To Dymphna) He's supposed to be.

BILLYGOAT

(To Hendryk) So are you to my thoughts as food to life.

HENDRYK

(To Billygoat) Stop it.
(To Esther) I've gained twenty-four pounds.

BILLYGOAT

Or as sweet seasoned showers are to the ground.

HENDRYK

Last night on the subway I urinated. In my pants.

BILLYGOAT

And as for the peace of you I hold such strife—

HENDRYK

(To Billygoat) SHUT UP! I hate the sonnets. Boring boring boring.

BILLYGOAT

. . . As 'twixt a miser and his wealth is found.

HENDRYK

I'm BROKE! I know women who have slept with you. New York is a tiny village. Well, it isn't but I do. I work with a woman who has. Slept with you.

ESTHER

No you don't.

HENDRYK

Yes I do.

ESTHER

No you don't.

HENDRYK

Yes I do. I know you're a lesbian.

ESTHER

And how does it make you feel.

HENDRYK

Sleep with me.

ESTHER

I'm going to charge you for this visit.

HENDRYK

I'll pay twice what I paid.

ESTHER

You're broke.

HENDRYK

I'll mug someone.

ESTHER

Ba-DUM-bump.
You keep saying "sleep" with me.

HENDRYK

Sex.

ESTHER

Sleep isn't sex.

HENDRYK

Nitpicker.

ESTHER

It's interesting.

HENDRYK

Kleinian nitpicker. I think you can sleep with me, uh, have sex with me because unlike the truly great analysts of the past who had unshakable faith in the stern tenets of their discipline, you and all modern practitioners of . . . well, of anything, of psychoanalysis in this instance, in our . . . um, *pickle*, conundrum, whatchamacallit, have, well, faith, but no unshakable faith, no one does in anything these days, we have . . . ambivalence, it's why we tattoo ourselves.

ESTHER

What?

HENDRYK

So like those priests who wind up sleeping with children, it's not their fault, I mean we should put them in prison of course, kill them probably, who knows. I know that's bad to say but there are days when everyone, um, seems like everyone should be killed, you know? In a world in which no structure rests assuredly, with assurancy on a foundation, in which nothing comes with a metaphysical guarantee, because even, take even an old atheist like Freud, God was still *watching*, He was *watching* all the way up until so-on-and-so-forth but today, today . . . Well take me for instance.
Only you have ever been watching me. For five years.
And nothing lasts longer than five years. Used to be, used to be . . . *ten* at least. And so abuse of your . . . of *one's* . . . wards, patients, *inferiors*, subjects. Well it's wrong but not absolutely so because there simply are no absolutes, and. The, uh.

ESTHER

I think the associative leap to tattoos is interesting.

HENDRYK

Tattoos last.

ESTHER

Your mother was tattooed.

HENDRYK

That again.

ESTHER

I am *absolutely* never going to sleep or have sex with you.

HENDRYK

Because I'm fat, urinate in my pants, and I'm broke. And frightening. I have a thought disorder.

ESTHER

I don't think you do.

HENDRYK

I think I do, but perhaps my thinking I do is a result of a thought disorder. If you think you have a thought disorder and you do have one, you're thinking a correct thought, in which case you don't have a thought *disorder.* So if I *don't* have a thought disorder, but think I do, *that is* a disorder, which means I *do* but then well you get the point. It's a small point. I saw a man with tattoos all over his body yesterday covering almost all his flesh like an epidermatological crisis. Now *that's* frightening. And I thought wow, the uh. Bet his skin will always smell like cheap ink. I thought, *wow*, the *pain,* he must've really enjoyed that suffering, bet he remembers every inky, little needle-stick. This is how he knows he's been here. Because it hurt to be. He has inscribed proof of his, well, not *existence* but . . . OK, sure, existence, sure, existence in, inscribed on his own, on his, in the only arena available to the late twentieth century citizen seeking effectivity, historical agency: his or her skin. I cannot

change any world except this small world which is bounded by my skin. I can change nothing, I can only hire a biker with a needle to bruise into my flesh, "Live Free or Die."
I'm scared. I'm scared of the world.
I really want to come back to you.
Maybe I'll get a tattoo.

(Pause.)

HENDRYK
Ambivalence expands our options. It increases our freedom, to, to . . . tattoo. Our selves. If we wish to. To have a concept like "our selves" or "my self." Which makes us more ambivalent and more free. Which drives us crazy, and makes us desperate to find nonambivalent things like tattoos which for all their permanence and pain serve mainly as markers of how ambivalent and impermanent we are. Or feel we are.

ESTHER
Actually tattoos are removable. Nowadays.

HENDRYK
I hate the way you introduce irrelevancies.

(Pause.)

HENDRYK
I have a boyfriend now.

ESTHER
That's good.

HENDRYK
He's beautiful and he has no soul. None. In nature there's no deformity but the mind. None are called evil but the unkind. Beauty's, um, good, a good thing, beauty is goodness, but the

Beauteous Evil are empty trunks o'erflourished by the whatchamacallit. The Devil. As they say.
I don't, I don't by the way believe that you are right that my mother named me Hendryk because it sounds like Schmendrik. SHE WAS *DUTCH*. FOR CHRIST'S SAKE! It's a *DUTCH NAME! NOT* . . . um, *NOT*. BECAUSE. IT SOUNDS. LIKE SCHMENDRIK. I don't think she meant that. I think that's wrong. I think you could be, uh I could sue you for malpractice for suggesting that, for, for, implanting, inscribing whatchamacallit, for forging neural pathways in my brain. Maternal ambivalence is lethal. You ruined my life.

ESTHER

But she *did* call you Schmendrik, Hendryk.

HENDRYK

SO?

ESTHER

She called you that all the time. It's Dutch but you were born in Massapequa. Schmendrik, Hendryk. The words are practically homonymic.

HENDRYK

Homophonous, actually, is what you—

ESTHER

Homonym and homophone are . . . homologues. They're homologous.

HENDRYK

They're homonyms, actually, not homologues, though homophony is the precise—

ESTHER

But if they're homonymous then they're precisely—

HENDRYK

Though there is a word more precisely connoting closeness but imprecision. But I can't remember what it is. Homophones are, like—

ESTHER

Tattoo and taboo.

HENDRYK

No, those aren't, they're, oh, ha ha.
My mom's favorite actor was Oskar Homolka. When she was angry she'd say, "What have you done, Oskar Homolka?" "Listen up, Oskar Homolka!" The subtext of the last minute is "homosexual." There I beat you to it. Pissed?
All this coil is long of you.
I want back in.
Tattoos are taboo for Jews. Taboo. It's . . . TABOOOOOO-OOOOOOOOOOoooooooooo. Like anal sex. I'm not a homosexual. I can't be. I have no talent to be. And anyway, the, uh. Anal sex disgusts me. Ugh. Anal sex. Ugh. I am filled with horror. Well that's too strong. Disgust.

BILLYGOAT

Do you know why that is?

HENDRYK

I don't know why it doesn't disgust everyone.

BILLYGOAT

But it doesn't.

HENDRYK

I don't know why.

BILLYGOAT

All sex has fragrance, and is sometimes malodorous. Love like Attar of Rose overwhelms with its fierce volatility the mephitic pungency of elimination and waste. When two lovers are conjoining. When my cock is up your butt.

HENDRYK

That is horribly horribly horribly embarrassing, what you just said, and I am going to vomit.

BILLYGOAT

Shit transforms.

HENDRYK

No it doesn't. It's irreducibly revolting. And germy. That is its essence. To revolt, and spread disease. You are very beautiful but you have no soul.

BILLYGOAT

Shit tranforms when you're in love.

HENDRYK

Maybe I've never been in love.

BILLYGOAT

Maybe not.

(Pause.)

HENDRYK

How . . . sad.

ESTHER

Schmendrik. I mean Hendryk.

HENDRYK

(To Esther) Waitaminnit.
(To Billygoat) But you love me.

BILLYGOAT

I do.

HENDRYK

But how is that possible? I mean, *look at me*? And you have no soul. I, I'm reasonably sure about that. You're a satyr. A Priapist. Nothing human is alien to you. It's inhuman.

BILLYGOAT

Having no soul makes a person indiscriminate. Makes it possible to fall in love with unworthy object choices, like you.

HENDRYK

But if I don't let you fuck me, you'll leave me.

DYMPHNA

I thought he was gone, I thought he terminated.

ESTHER

He asked to see me.

DYMPHNA

What's his real name?

(Pause.)

DYMPHNA

You shouldn't let him back.

ESTHER

I won't.

DYMPHNA

Ever. Promise.

ESTHER

Ever. Banished. Be gone.

HENDRYK

I don't understand.

BILLYGOAT

I have to leave you.

HENDRYK

But that's . . . that's *crazy.* You love me so much my shit smells like Attar of Rose. I mean I can't even say that without feeling nausea. But you say it does. But you're going to leave me if we don't fuck.

BILLYGOAT

Yes. Because your refusal means you don't love me. I know that's bad to say but we both know what the refusal means. You don't love me, Hendryk. And that breaks my heart. It makes me want to die.

HENDRYK

So if you leave me, you're going to die? Or are you just going to find a boyfriend who has no problems with the smell of Attar?

BILLYGOAT

Ummmm. The latter.

ESTHER

This morning I thought the bed was full of sand.

HENDRYK

I don't understand.

DYMPHNA

Is it bad today?

ESTHER

Hi-ho hi-ho it's off to work I go.
Yes, it's very very bad.

I want to die. God has closed my womb and I want to die. As a lesbian and a feminist and a rational progressive person and everything I am, as lucky as I am, I know it's bad to say this but I don't give a fuck. I am so fucking depressed I want to die. Die die die die die die die die. I want to have a baby. If I can't have a baby I want to die. I can't take any more of those pills, I don't want to get cancer; I don't want to superovulate I just want to have a baby so bad I want to die but I don't want cancer. But I really do want to die. I hate the baby that won't be born. I hate the five failed sperm donors. Inexplicably, I hate you. Certainly I hate myself. I can't describe the hatred I feel for the doctors who . . . I have projected the hatred I feel for those doctors and their superovulators onto my shrink and her antidepressants so I can't remember to take my Zoloft, which I need to do but I hate her and her Zoloft for seeking to rob me of my death-desiring depression which is now the only thing left of my baby. I don't believe in God, I never did, not even a little but my hate believes in God apparently and He has closed my womb so fuck you, God. While my patients are jabbering away on the couch I wish I had a big sand bucket like kids have at the beach and I imagine myself with a plastic shovel pouring sand in their jabbering mouths, slowly and deliberately and seriously the way kids do, filling their mouths with sand not just to *(To Hendryk)* SHUT THEM UP *(To Dymphna)* but obviously to strangle them; I wish all the world was burnt to a cinder, I wish I lived on the island of Montserrat. I do live on the island of Montserrat. You know that island with the . . . whatchamacallit, um, *volcano.* I imagine you calling my patients and saying, "Esther is dead, Dr. Zauber is dead, she killed herself, sorry, here are referrals." They would all be shocked and sad and so forth but also deeply gratified to have finally heard what you sound like, to have it confirmed that you exist, *my lover*. Parasites. Oy. Oy. Die. Die. Oy vey iz mir. Oh woe is me. Every morning's . . . I'm sorry, but it's only ever, "Oh no not *this* again." And know what? My complete lack of hope is all that keeps me alive. I think that if for one moment I felt hope, I would have the courage to kill myself. For real.

BILLYGOAT

(To Hendryk) There's always douching.

ESTHER

(To Hendryk) Did you ever play on the shore with a sand bucket?

HENDRYK

(To Esther) Why?
(To Billygoat) Douching isn't foolproof.

ESTHER

Just wondering.

BILLYGOAT

Ah, well, *foolproof.*

HENDRYK

I hate that.

BILLYGOAT

What?

HENDRYK

That continental wearywise affected sophisticated louche thing you lapse into. Ah well, foolproof. Americans don't say, "Ah." Ah well, foolproof. Ah well the smell of feces. In the faubourg of Paree of my youth we would eat it with petit pois off tiny platters of Limoges . . . Please. You're from Dearborne. In houses all across Dearborne mothers are teaching little boys to crinkle their noses in revulsion at the smell of ordure. Maybe they don't even need instruction, maybe it's innate, atavistic: poo-poo, yuck. What went wrong with you?

BILLYGOAT

With love's light wings did I oe'rperch that revulsion.

HENDRYK

You're so *robust*. You don't really *get* ambivalence. The satyr which is half man half goat should get ambivalence but animals don't, that's why we say they have no souls. Ambivalence is the soul, it is our species being, and against animal certitude human ambivalence is too ambivalent to stand up for itself I guess and so, voilà. You. I'm going to lie down now.

ESTHER

Time's almost up.

HENDRYK

(To Esther) Can I fuck you?

DYMPHNA

(To Esther) Can I fuck you?

BILLYGOAT

(To Hendryk) Can I fuck you?

ESTHER

(To Hendryk) No.
(To Dymphna) No fucking tonight.

BILLYGOAT

Don't let me leave you. I may not have a soul but I'm beautiful so do your soul a favor, hang on tight to me.

HENDRYK

I'm going to lie down now.

ESTHER

When you lie down on the couch you always pass out. Your efficient Resistance.

HENDRYK

Just for a . . . *(He lies down)* For old times' sake. To what? Why resist. I never met anyone who wasn't overcome. Eventually. The pillow always smells.

ESTHER

Many troubled heads have been laid upon it.
What about paternal ambivalence?

(Hendryk buries his face in the pillow and inhales deeply.)

ESTHER

What does it smell like, Hendryk?

HENDRYK

Attar. Of Something. Nice.
Not now I'm trying to sleep.
Thank you for seeing me. Aren't I sad? Paternal ambivalence, there's no such thing as that. My father lacked ambivalence. He hated me, till he figured out how to swallow me. Which he did in three snaps of his mighty jaws, and washed me down with beer. It hardly hurt. Him or me.
Once incorporated I was more or less safe and more or less whole.
And then extruded.
Spectacularly, lipsmackingly, invincibly unappetizing.
Maybe from this comes my horror at the thought of . . . the, uh.

(He's asleep.)

ESTHER

Hendryk.
Hendryk.
I have problems of my own.

DYMPHNA

Our inability to love one another is humankind's greatest tragedy. Why can't people live up to their moral goodness? It's better to share. It's more pleasant to be kind. Maybe not in the moment, but immediately after. It's exhausting to despair. Love replenishes itself, day after day. It's easy to love, it's hard to refuse. Surprises are always coming. Adversity is better met by good cheer and a placid spirit. Generosity makes us free. Sacrifice lifts the soul. For the happy woman there is no terror in the night. *Lass meine Schmerzen nicht verloren sein.* Let my sorrow and my pain not be in vain. Don't kill yourself. Work. Each evening come home to me. Surely goodness and mercy will follow me all the days of my life. I love that. Surely they shall. Surely. Surely.

ESTHER

Surely.
For me that word is so rotten with doubt and hesitation, it rings. It's a question in a closet.

DYMPHNA

Don't kill yourself. Work. Each evening come home to me.

(Esther takes the keys to her office out of her purse, scribbles something on a piece of paper. She wraps the keys in the paper, puts them quietly on the sleeping Hendryk's chest, turns out the lights and tiptoes out. Hendryk wakes up as the door shuts. He looks about. He sits up. The keys fall into his lap. He opens the paper in which they are wrapped. He jingles the keys. He reads the note.)

HENDRYK

Lock. Up. After. Yourself.

FINIS

East Coast Ode to Howard Jarvis

A Little Teleplay in Tiny Monologues

Howard Jarvis and the Anti-tax Revolution

HOWARD JARVIS (1903–1986), for those of you who hadn't been born when the self-styled "tax revolt leader" loomed on the Californian, and then the national, political horizon, managed to convince nearly two-thirds of the voters in the state to pass Proposition 13, which slashed property taxes by fifty-seven percent in 1978. Eventually the Jarvis warriors would claim that they managed to deprive the state budget of almost three hundred billion dollars in tax revenue (the consequences of which can be seen in California's impaupered education and health care systems, its unsheltered homeless, its untreated mental patients wandering its city streets). Jarvis and his Proposition sounded the first graceless klaxon battle-trumpet for the armies of neo-barbarians, massing under Reagan, preparing to shred the social net, and attempting to shred the Social Contract, finally offering to replace it, in 1995, with The Contract with America, the cornerstone of which was a reckless repealing of taxes.

America, ambivalently hoping for a functional society with decent public schools, affordable health care, breathable air and navigable highways, may be less eager to sign on the dotted line than Gingrich, now dismissed, and Jarvis, now largely forgotten, anticipated. People aren't always the mindless greedhogs the GOP believes them to be. Last year, in 1999, the Congressional Republicans offered a nearly eight hundred billion dollar tax cut, and were shocked to find that the national response was largely one of skepticism, annoyance and even indignation. But the anti-tax minotaurs are still stomping about, and in the wake of their efforts, valuable social programs have been cut, essential regulatory agencies have been whittled down to ineffectual size, public education is being starved and vouchered to death, the NEA has been reduced to the size of a nasty little joke, the income disparity gap between rich and poor is greater than it has ever been in our history, and we haven't hit bottom yet. If the GOP, and its collaborationists in the Democratic Party, have their way, we will.

Characters

Sixteen Men

THE CORRECTIONS OFFICER (African-American, thirties)

THE SKINHEAD INMATE (white, twenties)

A DETECTIVE, HOUSING POLICE, Charles Procaccino (Italian-American, thirties)

LEONARD "HAP" DUTCHMAN (white, fifties)

THE HOUSING DETECTIVE'S UNCLE, AN ACCOUNTANT (Italian-American, sixties)

THE SECOND DETECTIVE, HOUSING POLICE (Italian-American, thirties)

THE THIRD DETECTIVE, HOUSING POLICE (Latino, mid-forties)

A TRANSIT COP (Asian-American, twenties)

ENVIRONMENTAL PROTECTION OFFICER (Cuban-American, forties)

A PATROLMAN (young, fat, white guy)

A PRECINCT CAPTAIN (African-American, middle-aged)

SANITATION WORKER (Sikh-American)

A HANDSOME, YOUNG FIREMAN (white)

ATTORNEY FOR THE CITY OF NEW YORK (young Latino)

MAYOR, CITY OF NEW YORK

THE DEFENSE ATTORNEY FOR THE HOUSING DETECTIVES (Irish-American in his sixties)

Seven Women

THE HOUSING DETECTIVE'S DAUGHTER (Italian-American, teens)

THE SUPREMELY SCARY GIRL WHO KNOWS PRACTICALLY EVERYTHING (African-American, teens)

KAREN, THE HOUSING DETECTIVE'S DAUGHTER'S BEST FRIEND (Latina-American, teens)

THE WOMAN IN THE PAYROLL DEPARTMENT (African-American, early fifties)

A METER READER (middle-aged)

CITY SOCIAL WORKER (Asian-American, middle-aged)

UNITED STATES ATTORNEY (youthful forties)

And a cast of thousands (the screen subdividing).

The Action

The action takes place in New York City, beginning in 1991 and ending in 1996. This really happened, though not exactly as I imagined it step-by-step. The letter and several of the official responses at the end of the play are taken verbatim from newspaper accounts.

Author's Note

If performed onstage, I think this will work best with one actor playing all the parts. The actor could be a woman or a man. The interior and exterior titles, character descriptions and character identifications should be spoken by the actor before each character speaks. For example, when the play begins, the actor will say:

ACTOR

> Interior shot. Rikers Island Jail. In his thirties, African-American, jail-guard uniform. A Corrections Officer. I guess I have always felt I pay too much taxes. Right? And I'm like, *for what*? Two days ago . . . etc.

The different characters should be gently suggested, with slight indications of accent and gender; the play shouldn't become a cacophony of funny voices, fake mustaches and drag acting.

Thanks to Alec Baldwin for commissioning this.

Thanks to Tess Timoney for the Spanish.

Interior Shot—Rikers Island Jail

In his thirties, African-American, jail-guard uniform.

THE CORRECTIONS OFFICER

I guess I have always felt I pay too much taxes. Right? And I'm like, *for what*? Two days ago I'm like waiting *twenty-seven minutes* for a subway train, middle of the day, and I'm like, I'm *late*, I'm like, "Come *on* man I pay all these fucking taxes like, for *this*?" For this *shit*? *Right*? Death, taxes and the fucking Mass Transit Authority. That *sucks*. That ain't right, right? I mean there must be more to life, you know what I mean?

So one day about five years ago at Rikers, I work over at Rikers, we got this weird skinhead white kid grand larceny assault or something, serious mental event, serious attitude problem, *nasty*, first day there he shoves some other prisoner on line at the cafeteria or he changed the channels on the TV without asking permission or I forget what but like so I have to take him to see the psychiatrist, get him some of them anti-aggression pills. I wait with him while he waits to see the doctor, and he's a talker.

Interior Shot—Rikers Island

In his twenties, generic white guy, shaved head with stubble, tattoos, prisoner coveralls.

THE SKINHEAD INMATE

. . . this secret group which I can't tell you the name of but to which I belong, the initials of which are N. A. W. . . . uh . . .

Wait, N. A. W. *(He mouths the words North American White Men's Freedom and Liberty Council silently, gleaning the capitals as he goes, then)* The N. A. W. M. F. and L. C. . . . And we have grokked this shit but *profoundly*, like you probably *think* I am in jail here but I am not in jail in my own mind, like . . . That's *Thoreau*! Leonard, he reads *Thoreau*! And he gots us some Uzis, we got Khlashnishnikov . . . Klashkhalnikov . . . Kaklishni . . . whatever, those Russian Uzis, and AK-47s, zebra bullets, dum-dums, Semtex . . . Man. The free mind, the superior mind overturns the system. Leonard, Leonard is like the mastermind, he is so smart *(Confidingly, sotto voce)* he doesn't pay taxes. No shit, he hasn't paid taxes in twenty years and it's *legal* because Leonard has proved through Thoreau and shit like that that the IRS is unconstitutional. I mean it man, clean and sober. No taxes. I have seen his paycheck.

Exterior Shot—On the Street, Bensonhurst

In his late thirties, Italian-American, tanned, pomaded hair, gold chain, amulets, a police ID badge; he is wearing a fancy Nike sweatsuit.

A DETECTIVE, HOUSING POLICE

So the skinhead fruitcake tells the corrections officer this guy Leonard has found a legal way out of paying taxes.

(Beat)

But apparently he won't give the officer this Leonard guy's number or nothing because the officer's black and Leonard lives out in Indiana where I guess there are only white people, anyway, I mean who the fuck's ever even *heard* of Indiana, I mean name-me-one-city-in-Indiana-you-got-two-seconds-bleep-time's-up—five-to-one this skinhead kid's never even made it out to Coney Island, *Indiana,* Jesus *wept*. He hooked up with *(Making "quotation marks" gestures with his fingers)* "Leonard" on the Internet . . . Now tell me please who is it teaching disturbed individuals like this bonebrain how to get on the fucking *Internet.* Like when I first heard the story I didn't even know what the Internet *was* let alone how to *(Gestures again)* "get on it" but here's this little cheap-ass racist loon got himself on the Internet and he's cooked up this whole fantasy about Indiana where allegedly they got something he called the North American White Men's Freedom and Liberty Council. I heard all this from a friend of mine over at Rikers knows a guy who knows this guy who got it from this kid: some bunch of armed whackos in Indiana who had figured out how legally to get out of paying taxes.

(Beat. He taps his noggin with his forefinger: "Bright idea!" Big smile, shaking his head) MotheraGod. Gonna get me some of *that.*

Interior Shot—Teenage Girl's Bedroom, Bensonhurst

Seriously disaffected youth, hair in cornrows, dreads, beaded, braided, dyed, mohawked, scalped; ear and nose piercings, tattoos.

THE HOUSING DETECTIVE'S DAUGHTER

My dad is always trying to win the lottery and shit, get-rich-quick ideas, it's pathetic, like, you can just *look* at him and see, "This guy is gonna get rich? Ever? No *way.*" I mean he does OK and all he just looks like a buttwipe. He all the time implies that I am stupid like he asks me what the Internet is. And he says can I find some stupid group on the Web for him, like, *Dad, I* am the first of my friends who found totally naked pictures of Antonio Banderas (like you can see everything it is so *gross*), so of course yes I know how to get on the Internet, buttwipe. Not to his face of course but I know how to call him buttwipe with just my facial expression, so he can get mad all he likes but he cannot hit me. Which if I *literally* called him buttwipe, he could. So he gives me this piece of paper with North American White Men's Freedom and Liberty Council, so I'm like, "*Whatever.*" Buttmunch. So I did some superlative prizewinning grass with my best friend Karen and we got on the Web Crawler in the school library and fed it the name of this stupid group, and *nada*, so we tried unlinking the words, like give us anything with North plus American plus White plus Men plus Freedom, and of course there were a zillion entries for that so like no way forget that. So Dad said try "Leonard" which was so gigantically lame, what a Cro-Magnon Pleistocene Pathetic Troglodyte Fossilized Freeze-Dried Buttmunch, but I told him if he gave me ten bucks I would try "Leonard," so he did so I bought some more grass for Karen and me and some brewskis and some Camel Lights and she had some Ecstasy and some Crystal Meth already and we typed in "Leonard" and the Web Crawler was like, "Duh?" So we were like *(Throat-slitting gesture)* "DOOMSDAY!" but then we asked this *supremely* scary girl at school who knows practically *everything*.

Exterior Shot—The Front Steps of a Public High School in Bensonhurst

An African-American teenager, very cool, supremely self-possessed, dressed in perfect B-Girl style.

THE SUPREMELY SCARY GIRL
WHO KNOWS PRACTICALLY EVERYTHING

What the fuck is the North American White Men's . . . Man, how the fuck should *I* know? Sounds to me like one of those militia groups they got out there, them head-job freaks who dynamited that federal building a few years ago in Utah or wherever.

Interior—Teenage Girl's Bedroom, Bensonhurst

THE HOUSING DETECTIVE'S DAUGHTER

So I told my dad who after all is a cop what this girl said, that these guys might be like terrorists or something, so he goes, "So give me back my ten bucks." Pathetic, no? We tried "Militias" but there was a zillion entries, and "Utah" but again a zillion entries, it would have taken us hours— and *then* because I am a genius and because I did not want to give him his ten bucks back I thought "Bombs, *guns* . . . lightbulb!" So Karen and me tried "Guns" and got a zillion entries and then tried "Semiautomatic Weapons" and got a thousand entries and then "Semis" plus "Liberty" and got maybe forty entries, and so that's how we went shopping for "Leonard" in Cyberspace.

Interior Shot—High School Library

A teenage Latina, dressed similarly to the detective's daughter.

KAREN, HER BEST FRIEND

We found the Web address for this North American White Zombie Psycho Brigade or whatever they call it, I forget, it was listed in this Online 'zine called, um, "Hyper-Vigilance!" or something. H-T-T-P-colon-slash-slash-W-W-W-dot-TEA-PARTY-dot-com. So she tells her pappi she found it, and he gives her another ten bucks and tells her, E-mail them asking them do they know how he can get out of paying his taxes. And this dude is a *cop*. So she's goin', let's send this guy, Leonard "Hap" Dutchman, let's send him the E-mail, but I'm goin' wait, Sondra, you better come up with a better screen name 'cause you been using your real last name and these guys is loco crazy and you could get your pappi in trouble and anyway your last name is Procaccino and to these guys that ain't gonna sound white enough. So we tried to think up the whitest name we could think of and I remembered the name from off this book from school last year which no one in the whole class even bothered to read.

Exterior Shot—An Indiana Cornfield

Generic white guy, fifties, fat, combat fatigues, militia cap, vaguely sinister toothbrush mustache, big smile.

LEONARD "HAP" DUTCHMAN

Dear Ethan Frome:
Thank you for writing to the North American White Men's Freedom and Liberty Council. I applaud your interest in waging a counterstrike against the tyranny of taxation, imposed upon free individuals such as yourself and myself by the Zionist Occupation Government HQ'd in D.C., its agents the Revenue Service and its armed forces of occupation otherwise known as the Bureau of Tobacco Drugs and Firearms and their elite corps the so-called United States so-called Marshalls. To *paraphrastically* quote our ancestral predecessor freeman John Paul Jones, "Won't fire till you see the eyes of our whites!" *(He laughs)*
Having never before tested the tax-rebellion waters as far east as Tel Aviv—pardon me I mean New York City, I counsel initially a low-key tactical maneuver, to wit: Request from your payroll office a W-4 form. When you receive it, in the blank space provided for "exemptions" write the number "98," hurling all the while appropriate imprecations and oaths against the high-handed shekel-mongering armed moneygrubbering rug-merchants who force you survilely to beg for "exemptions" from *their* usurious theft of *your* hard-earned dollars. There's *no* I repeat *no* legal limit to the number of "exemptions" a citizen can claim, so claim "98," which if granted will effectively and *legally* lift from your stooped-but-proud shoulders the oppressors' contumely, also known as your entire tax bill; and if your claim is initially rejected, repeat the process several times, and if that don't work, Ethan, E-mail me for further instructions. In the meantime I will Cyber-send you various useful items including literature and a membership application for the

National Rifle Association. Good luck, fellow patriot, oh, and Happy Hermann Goering's Birthday, Mr. Frome! *(He gives a little Hitler salute)*

Interior—A Cluttered Accountant's Office, Bensonhurst

A harried, little, Italian-American guy in his sixties, shirt and tie, glasses, long nose hairs.

THE HOUSING DETECTIVE'S UNCLE, AN ACCOUNTANT

My nephew-in-law asks me is it OK he files *98* exemptions on his W-4, *what* 98 exemptions, of course not you idiot. I tell him 98 exemptions you wouldn't be paying any taxes, right he tells me that's the point, I tell him listen Charlie remember Ernest Hemingway you do not want to worry the IRS is after you, not unless you like the idea of going down on a double-barrel shotgun *(He mimes with mid- and forefinger the aforementioned act, cocks his thumb as if pulling a trigger) BOOM!* Pay your taxes you're a goddamn cop already, what is this supposed to be a free lunch a, a, a free ride, *98 tax exemptions* what is you a friggin' communist, gimme a friggin' break. Moron!

Interior—The Payroll Office at One Police Plaza

A pleasant-looking African-American woman in her early fifties, office dress.

THE WOMAN IN THE PAYROLL DEPARTMENT

The first time I saw it I thought it was a mistake, or a joke so I sent it back. He sends it in again, 98 exemptions. I circled 98 in a red pen and a question mark and I sent it back. He sends it in again. 98 exemptions. I show it to my supervisor who between us is usually 98 *proof* before lunchtime, bottle's in his desk, lower left-hand drawer. He can't even *focus* so he stamps it *ITEMIZE,* so I send it back to the detective stamped *ITEMIZE.* I figure at least this'll be good for a laugh.

Interior—Headquarters of the North American White Men's Freedom and Liberty Council

LEONARD "HAP" DUTCHMAN

Dear Ethan:
As per itemization, try our secret weapon: download and append the attached letter to your W-4 form. This document has proven highly effective by your fellow resistance fighters out here in the ZOG-free liberation zone formerly known as Crawfordsville. Please do not share this letter with anyone you do not love as a brother, nor with any women be they wives or mothers, nor I hardly need mention with members of other races. Happy hunting, Ethan, oh, and for twenty-five dollars you can obtain an autographed copy *(He holds up a book)* of my annotated edition of Mr. Henry David Thoreau's survivalist manifesto *On Walden Pond. God* bless you and your progeny!
(He starts to sing:)
BORN FREE,
As free as the wind blows,
As free as the grass grows . . .

A DETECTIVE, HOUSING POLICE

(Reading from a letter:)
To The Treasury Department:
Regarding Internal Revenue Service Publication 519 and 515. I submit the following statement in duplicate stating all my natural rights without prejudice in order to obtain work and not to be subject to withholding. I declare that I am an

American man now in an area known geographically as New York. I was not born in the District of Columbia nor any possession or territory thereof. I do not inhabit the forum of your jurisdiction known as the United States as defined within the Internal Revenue Code. I am not a citizen or resident of any state or federal conglomerate within your jurisdiction. All remunerations for labor are received from sources outside the United States and are not connected to trade or business within the United States. Since I am alien to the United States, and am not a resident there, I am therefore a nonimmigrant nonresident alien to the United States. I have never filed Form 1078 as prescribed that would rebut my nonresidence status. I never had any income attributable to 26 USC 872 Subsection (a), Subsection (1) or Subsection (2). I am excluded from having to obtain and submit an identifying number to you. Should I have any income from within the United States . . .

THE WOMAN IN THE PAYROLL DEPARTMENT

(Reading:)

". . . I am still not subject to withholding of any kind of said income as it is not deemed to be income. I am not within a state or the United States, nor am I a person, individual or taxpayer. Signed, Charles Procaccino, Detective, Housing Police, City of New York."

(She puts the letter down)

The United States of America. Lemme tellya.

I read the letter a few times. Alien to the United States. Baby, I hear what you're saying. I am fifty-one years old. My apartment is a box. I got no money, I hate my job, I hate this city, I hate my cat, my husband hates his job, this city, the cat, we hate the disappointments, the delays in construction, the bigots, the bozos, the Democrats *and* the Republicans, Newt Gingrich, Bill Clinton, *his* cat, Rudy Giuliani, my insurance company and my boss, the guy playing with himself on the subway at 9 A.M., the kid with the radio playing at 6 A.M. and I hate the piss smell in the hallway that I have to inhale. Every day. On my way. To my box. Where I *live.* AND the fluorescent light fixtures they put up ten years ago in this office where I work that for ten years have been going *Buuuuzzzzzzzzzzzz* all the livelong day like to drive me *CRAZY.*

I xeroxed the letter and I sent it to my supervisor and on to the IRS folks in Huntington, sent it to Albany, uptown, down-town, all around the town, put it in the detective's file, totaled up 98 *itemized* exemptions and where it says "Federal With-holding" I entered "zero" and State Withholding I entered "zero" and cut him his big fat check with no taxes withheld and sent in on, let *them* sort it out it is *not* my problem. You and me pal, Aliens to the United States. I'd try it myself—if I was crazy and stupid and looking to get pitched in jail. But God bless the child. He got his own.

Exterior Shot—The Staten Island Ferry Terminal

Italian-American, mid-thirties, suit and tie.

THE SECOND DETECTIVE, HOUSING POLICE

I thought he was just, you know, crazy or stupid. Then a few months later he shows me a bunch of his pay stubs: "No Taxes Withheld." He showed me the letter. I read it sixty times. I am a smart guy and I cannot understand a word, he explains it sixty times and I still cannot understand a word, I can smell *bullshit* when it is waved under my nose but I cannot under-stand the letter. I never been to Indiana, I don't read the papers, I've never read Thoreau, I know nobody ever needed an Uzi to hunt deer or whatever kind of animal they hunt in Indiana so I don't know what this Leonard character is up to but those pay stubs, *that* I can understand. That is my kind of reading material. Three pay stubs that read like that and I'm gonna buy myself a motherflippin' home entertainment center!

Exterior—Night, in Front of the Giant Coca-Cola Sign, Times Square

A Latino man, mid-forties, police uniform.

THE THIRD DETECTIVE, HOUSING POLICE

I sort of feel taxes are . . . Well people have been paying taxes since . . . civilization, really, I mean since it began, because, well, it costs money to, to *have* a civilization and we don't want to be . . . um, barbarians or . . . I remember back in the sixties we . . . People talked then about not paying their taxes but it was like . . . Well, the war and all, different, different times. Plus which also I am an officer. Of the *Law*. But. Well. By the time it got around to me there were already six, seven, *ten* guys all pulling in three times . . . well, *twice* as much as before because . . . A *lot* gets deducted, so anyway. *(He shakes his head, confused)* I'm confused. Why did I . . . ? I dunno. Seemed like a good idea at the time? Money pressure? Peer pressure? Nostalgia? *(Leans forward, raises a little power fist, speaks softly)* Ho Chi Minh! Be Like Him! Dare to struggle! Dare to win! Remember? *(Mimes toking on a joint, makes a little peace sign, grins blissfully)* Remember that?
There is no force as great as an idea whose time has come.

Exterior—Underneath the El Tracks, 125th Street and Broadway

An Asian-American man in his twenties, uniform.

A TRANSIT COP

When Jesus says render unto Caesar that which is Caesar's and unto God what belongs to God this is it seems to me a very, very deliberately ambiguous statement. Jesus is *carefully* avoiding specifying what exactly it is which belongs to Caesar, or if, in point of fact, *anything* really does.

Exterior—The Brooklyn Naval Yard Incinerator

Cuban-American man in his forties.

ENVIRONMENTAL PROTECTION OFFICER

Me dice que hay cuarenta policias de housing que estan ya metidos, quisas veinte policias de transito, como veinte en Port Authority, EPO, me enseña sus pay stubs. Era un detective en housing yo creo, es *encreible*, ningun impuesto, *no taxes*, y me dice que me puede vender un packete que me explica todo, me costaria novecientos dolares . . .
(Translation: He tells me forty housing cops are in on it already, maybe twenty transit cops, twenty or so over at Port Authority, EPO, he shows me his pay stubs, he was, uh, a detective in housing I think, it's like incredible, no taxes, no taxes, and he says he can sell me a packet, self-explanatory, it would cost me nine hundred bucks . . .)

Interior—A Locker Room, Police Plaza Gym

A young, fat, white guy, in a sweatsuit.

A PATROLMAN

I do not inhabit the forum of your jurisdiction known as the United States as defined within the Internal Revenue Code. I am not a citizen or resident of any state or federal conglomerate within your jurisdiction.

Exterior—Night, Little Italy, San Gennaro Procession

A middle-aged, African-American man.

A PRECINCT CAPTAIN

I am still not subject to withholding of any kind of said income as it is not deemed to be income.

Interior—Living Room of an Apartment in Washington Heights

A middle-aged woman in brown traffic cop clothes.

A METER READER

I am therefore a nonimmigrant, nonresident, Alien to the United States. I have never filed Form 1078. I never had any income attributable to 26 USC 872 Subsection (a), Subsection (1) or Subsection (2) . . .

Interior—Rikers Island

The same Corrections Officer as at the beginning.

THE CORRECTIONS OFFICER

But what burns my ass is, like, I had to pay the mother two thousand dollars for his tax "packet" and I *know* it did not cost him no two thousand to write "98" on a blank W-4 form and xerox this fucked-up letter that don't make no kind of sense. So why I got to pay two thousand dollars when half the force is doing this and they didn't have to pay *nothing*?! That is not right. I was thinking of reporting his ass but then I decided against it, choosing instead to amortize the two grand as an unavoidable business expense spread over the course of two or three of these here Paychecks Blown Down From Paradise. Lookee this here! *(He shows the paycheck) Ain't that phat!* I am taking my kids to Disney World!

Interior—Headquarters of the North American White Men's Freedom and Liberty Council

LEONARD "HAP" DUTCHMAN

Dear Ethan Frome:

We are pleased to hear that your East Coast rebellion is proceeding apace. I must warn you however against spreading the good news too liberally, if you catch my meaning.

(The screen subdivides into many little boxes, each containing the smiling face of one of the officers we've met so far.)*

LEONARD "HAP" DUTCHMAN

Because patriot Frome if there are too many nonimmigrant, nonresidents residing in one location it could bring the wrath of ZOG down upon us all . . .

(The screen further subdivides into many, many, many little boxes, multitudes of happy city employees who aren't paying taxes. Lines of static flash across the screen, the reception falters.)

LEONARD "HAP" DUTCHMAN

. . . and we do not I repeat do *not* want to face the wrath of ZOG before our tax rebellion has rendered it sufficiently cash-starved and weakened so the Council cautions you to . . .

(The screen goes blank and is instantly filled with a notice:)

THIS WEB SITE IS TEMPORARILY UNAVAILABLE.

Exterior Shot—The Statue of Liberty

A Sikh-American sanitation worker in a splendid turban.

SANITATION WORKER

I am a nonimmigrant nonresident Alien to the United States.

Interior—Bellevue Psychiatric Ward

A middle-aged Asian-American woman, blouse and skirt.

CITY SOCIAL WORKER

I was not born in the District of Columbia nor any possession or territory thereof, and my natural rights . . .

*If performed theatrically, the following could be accomplished with slides.

Exterior—Outside a Burning Building, Upper West Side

A HANDSOME YOUNG FIREMAN

I am not within a state or the United States, nor am I a person, individual or taxpayer. Thank you very, *very* much in advance for your prompt cooperation in ceasing to withhold my taxes! *(Smiles)*

Interior—Cubicle, Office of Comptroller, Lower Manhattan

Young Latino man, glasses, suit and tie.

ATTORNEY FOR THE CITY OF NEW YORK

Dear Sir or Madam:
Please be advised that the status you are seeking as "nonresident nonimmigrant Alien" does not exist nor is it recognized by any local, state or federal tax code or statute.

(Cut to: The Housing Detective, staring in open-mouthed incredulity. Cut back to:)

ATTORNEY FOR THE CITY OF NEW YORK

Dear Sir or Madam:
Your request for "nonresident or nonimmigrant Alien" status has been denied inasmuch as no such status exists. Please be informed by this that you appear to be in arrears for federal income-, social security withholding-, state income-, state unemployment insurance-, and local withholding *taxes.*

(Cut to:)

A DETECTIVE, HOUSING POLICE

Dear City of New York:
As a, uh, sovereign individual, who hereby formally declares himself to be a separate legal entity, one nation, as it were, indi-

visible, or rather, to quote from that classic of American tax resistance, *On Walden Pond* . . .

(Cut to:)

THE SECOND DETECTIVE, HOUSING POLICE

We declare that taxation without representation is unconstitutional and we do not feel represented by the governments in question and as it says in the Declaration of Independence which *we* spell I-N-D-E-P-E-N-D-E-N-T-S as in I am independent of your authority to request . . .

(Cut to:)

ATTORNEY FOR THE CITY OF NEW YORK

Dear Mr. Martinez, Mr. Austin, Mr. Yow, Mr. Shabaka, Officer Vanuzzi, Officer Vasquez, Sergeant McGuire, Miss Lefkowitz, Detective Pentangelo, Captain Russlowski, Mrs. Nguyen . . .

(Cut to:)

A DETECTIVE, HOUSING POLICE

Uh, Dear Leonard . . .

(Screen message:)

THIS WEB SITE IS TEMPORARILY UNAVAILABLE.

(Cut to:)

CITY SOCIAL WORKER

Dear City of New York, Dear State of New York, Dear Treasury Department:

I do not recognize your letter. I do not recognize you. I am not a person nor an individual nor a taxpayer. You have no jurisdiction over me. Paying taxes is *voluntary*. Had I realized this before I would never have paid any taxes, and I have been paying taxes, before this year of my dawning realization that I could not legally be compelled, I have paid taxes for seventeen years: I am *not* in arrears—*YOU* OWE *ME* MONEY!

Interior—Teenage Girl's Bedroom, Bensonhurst

THE HOUSING DETECTIVE'S DAUGHTER

So like H-T-T-P-slash-slash-W-W-W-dot-TEAPARTY-dot-com was like permanently *fried*, so we went back to Hyper-Vigilance, the online 'zine, and they had this whole article about how Leonard had been busted in Cincinnati for crossing state lines with a suitcase fulla Uzis, and some bullets, and also he wrote some letter to a U.S. Marshall saying he was gonna whack him or something.

Interior—Maximum Security Prison Cell, Federal Penitentiary, Toledo, Ohio

LEONARD "HAP" DUTCHMAN

(Singing:)
To dream the impossible dream
To love pure and chaste from afar
To strive when your arms are too weary . . .
(Prison bars slam across the screen, Leonard behind them)*
To reach the Unreachable STAR!
THIS IS MY QUEST!
TO FOLLOW THAT STAR
NO MATTER HOW HOPELESS . . .

*Slides again, or a sound effect.

(Under song dissolve to:)

Interior—U.S. Attorney's Office, Briefing Room

A press conference, mikes at a podium, the U.S. Attorney, a forty-year-old woman in a power suit.

UNITED STATES ATTORNEY

Our preliminary computer check indicates that as few as five hundred and as many as a thousand city workers have been involved in this tax evasion scheme, some for as long as five years. Scores of law enforcement officers seem to be involved . . .

Interior—Manhattan Courtroom

The Housing Detective in a suit and tie, looking haggard. A gavel is banging.

DETECTIVE, HOUSING POLICE

I have no quarrel with this court, Your Honor. I am here against my wishes. I have no standing in this court. And the court has no jurisdiction over me.

Exterior—Steps of City Hall, Manhattan

An out-of-doors press conference, mikes and a podium. The mayor, a shifty-looking, snaggle-toothed guy with furtive close-set eyes, a bellicose speaking style and a bad comb-over.

MAYOR, CITY OF NEW YORK

This isn't uh ideological. This is pure out-and-out cheating. This is a way of cheating and not paying your taxes by people who are sworn to uphold the Constitution of the United States. If they were ideologically concerned, uh, *political*, uh, that is to say, making some sort of statement, they, uh, well they could have quit their jobs, rather than try to cheat the United States and the state out of taxes. They should have just quit!

Interior Shot—A Classroom for Smart Kids, Bensonhurst Public School

THE SUPREMELY SCARY GIRL WHO KNOWS PRACTICALLY EVERYTHING

(Giving a report) The Social Contract. The Social Contract is a theory *propounded (Big smile, she's proud of that word)* by Thomas Hobbes, John Locke and Jean-Jacques Rousseau, who were French philosophers. Um, part of the deal is, like, the people agree to surrender their power to the state. Some of their power. But it's like, *how much*? And it's like, say you the state and I'm the people, did I "lend" you my power and can I fire you if I don't like what you doing with my power, or am I just born as a citizen alienated from my power, did I somehow give up my power at birth and now I just got to hope for the best from you, and um, oh yeah: like, is this a contract between authority and each individual or is it, like, a collective expression of a general will towards civilization?

Interior—A Plush Law Firm Conference Room

Set up to meet the press. A weary Irish-American man in his sixties. Rumpled, expensive suit, glasses.

THE DEFENSE ATTORNEY FOR THE HOUSING DETECTIVES

But no, no, it's really not ideological, I wouldn't call what my clients did *ideological*, I . . . What's that? Uh, well. I would call it more like . . . Uh, well, idiocy. Or lunacy. Take your pick.

Interior—Payroll Office at One Police Plaza

THE WOMAN IN THE PAYROLL DEPARTMENT

The day they announced they'd commenced to arrest those people was the day that TWA plane blew up and fell from the sky. I'm not a superstitious woman, but sometimes there are signs, you know, warnings, you know what I mean, writing on the wall. Not that anybody knows how to read anymore, not that anyone's looking up at the wall to read the writing, but, you know . . . Signs. Trouble ahead. Oh, and Wall Street had a REAL bad day that day because the unemployment rate had gone *down.* That's what it said: the price of stocks fell 'cause there was too many people who had jobs. So I suppose that means stocks will go back up when enough people get fired?
My supervisor got fired, for gross incompetence, and I'm thinking of going for his job. Get my own cubicle, that way. Privacy. Maybe I'll start to drink.
Death and taxes. Baby . . .
I don't know what they're gonna do to those poor stupid people. You could draw some bad inferences from all this. Things coming unglued. Can't blame the little criminals too much. Things coming unglued, that's how it seems to me. Don't it seem like that to you?
Everything's just coming apart at the seams.
And nobody understands.

(President Clinton delivering the punchline of his 1996 *State of the Union Speech before both houses of Congress.)*

PRESIDENT CLINTON

So I join with Congress and my fellow Americans in declaring: The Era of Big Government Is Over!

(Cheers as the screen fades to black.)

THE END

TONY KUSHNER's plays include *A Bright Room Called Day*, *Angels in America* (Parts One and Two) and *Slavs!*; as well as adaptations of Corneille's *The Illusion*, Ansky's *The Dybbuk*, Brecht's *The Good Person of Szechuan* and Goethe's *Stella*. Current projects include two plays: *Homebody/Kabul* and *Henry Box Brown or The Mirror of Slavery*; and two musical plays: *St. Cecilia or The Power of Music* and *Caroline or Change*. He is collaborating with Maurice Sendak on an American version of the children's opera, *Brundibar*. Mr. Kushner has been awarded a Pulitzer Prize for Drama, two Tony Awards, the Evening Standard Award, an OBIE, the New York Drama Critics Circle Award, an American Academy of Arts and Letters Award, and a Whiting Writers Fellowship, among other awards; recently he received a Lila Wallace/Reader's Digest Fellowship and a medal for Cultural Achievement from the National Foundation for Jewish Culture. He grew up in Lake Charles, Louisiana, and he lives in New York.